# Songs on the Journey

# Songs on the Journey

Life, love & laughter in a Bible translation project

Robin McKenzie

Songs on the Journey
Published by Wycliffe Bible Translators NZ
PO Box 276005
Manukau City
Auckland 2241
New Zealand

www.wycliffenz.org
admin@wycliffenz.org

© 2023 Robin McKenzie
Copyright of the songs that appear in this book
belongs to Robin & Delwyn McKenzie.

ISBN 978-0-473-68282-8 (Softcover)
ISBN 978-0-473-68283-5 (ePUB)
ISBN 978-0-473-68284-2 (Kindle)

Production & Typesetting:
Andrew Killick
Castle Publishing Services
www.castlepublishing.co.nz

Cover Design:
Paul Smith

Scriptures taken from
the Holy Bible, New International Version®, NIV®.
Copyright © 1973, 1978, 1984, 2011 by Biblica, Inc.™
Used by permission of Zondervan.
All rights reserved worldwide.

ALL RIGHTS RESERVED

No part of this publication may be reproduced,
stored in a retrieval system, or transmitted
in any form or by any means, electronic, mechanical,
photocopying, recording or otherwise,
without prior written permission from the author.

# Contents

| | | |
|---|---|---|
| Preface | | 7 |
| Acknowledgements | | 11 |
| 1. | Stuck in the Mud | 13 |
| 2. | Steep Learning Curves | 23 |
| 3. | A Dark Cloud | 39 |
| 4. | New Trail, New Village, New Home | 49 |
| 5. | Christmas Guests | 61 |
| 6. | A Song in the Night | 71 |
| 7. | Bridges Built, Damaged, Repaired | 77 |
| 8. | In Sickness and Health | 87 |
| 9. | A Family Visit | 97 |
| 10. | Questions | 107 |
| 11. | Writing Competition | 119 |
| 12. | The Miry Clay | 131 |
| 13. | New Countries | 161 |
| 14. | Davao | 177 |
| 15. | Translation | 187 |
| 16. | Grieving | 199 |
| 17. | House to House | 213 |
| 18. | New Songs | 225 |
| 19. | Everywhere Has Its Challenges | 237 |
| 20. | Through the Waters, Through the Fire | 245 |

| | | |
|---|---|---|
| 21. | Final Checks | 253 |
| 22. | New Testament Dedication | 261 |

Epilogue 269

Appendix 1: Maps 273
Appendix 2: Songs 279

# Preface

Growing up in a church with a strong missions focus, Delwyn felt a call to serve overseas from the age of nine. My own heart was not stirred in that direction until after we were married, though I had been part of a short-term missions trip to Fiji a few years earlier. We have both loved reading missions biographies. Along with a time of concerted prayer and fasting as to life direction, several of them were instrumental in birthing in me an excitement for missions and directing our steps towards Bible translation. My hope in writing this account is that it may spur others toward serving the Lord, if not along a similar track, then along another God-directed path as He leads their steps.

First, though, the impetus to begin writing this account was from our children, who each lived through at least the major part of this time period, but whose memories are somewhat fragmented. They got on my case to record all that happened because recollections of the many trips in and out of the village began to merge. 'Nagged' is probably too strong a word, but 'suggested' is decidedly too weak. They therefore get part of the blame, though they would no doubt rather take all of the credit.

Although I have written the bulk of this account, I could not have done so without Delwyn's letters home to her mother (which her mother kept in a clear file binder "for when you write your book"). Even more valuable was Delwyn's journal. Many of the facts I could recall from memory or from pointers in 'RADISH',* our occasional newsletter. But the heart of the story, the emotions behind the facts, and the recorded prayers and answers are from her journals. I did not realise before I read them just how stressful some of our experiences were for her. (Though I know I was stressed at many points too.) Now, having read them, I feel I know my wife better than ever and I am even more proud to have such a courageous woman by my side. In the course of this account, I frequently refer to excerpts from her journals (written in italics) to give her perspective on whatever we were facing at the time.

While the italicised sections are integral to the storyline, there are also some boxed sections that provide background material, some of which gives a little basic insight into linguistic and/or translation principles. If such information is not of interest to you, just jump over it and carry on reading.

When first mooting the idea of writing this story, my working title was: 'Head in the Clouds, Feet in the Mud.' This was appropriate in that we were often full of bright ideas while ignorant of all that was involved and at times felt like we were getting nowhere. Its less metaphorical meaning referred to the quagmires on the trips in and out, and the ever-present smoke in the villages. In the end we opted for an alternative.

*Songs on the Journey* seemed to us an appropriate title, in that this particular slice of our life's journey was filled with songs. There were the known songs written by others that were fitting or encouragements at various points—songs like Don Moen's: 'God Will Make a Way'. There were songs that Delwyn was inspired to write in response to the challenges we were facing or the prayers of our hearts. There were songs

---

* 'Robin And Delwyn's Illustrated Send-Home'

written for school musicals that were meaningful to us at other times as well. And there were the Scripture songs in the Tabulahan language that Delwyn composed, several of which were in a traditional Tabulahan style. A number of these original songs are footnoted at relevant points throughout the book and incorporated as sheet music in Appendix 2, where there is also a QR code and web link to audio versions.

I have read many missions biographies and been inspired time and again by the calibre of the people in facing tremendous odds, their walk with God, the miraculous answers to prayer and the wonderful results of their ministries. It is easy to think of such men and women as super saints, and missionaries often tend to be put on a pedestal in their home churches. In reality, they are all ordinary men and women, simply making themselves available for however God wants to use them.

This story is not like many of the missions biographies I have read. We weren't facing the tremendous challenges of so many early missionaries. Though there are answers to prayer recorded here, it is not a record of one miraculous event after another. It is simply one family's account of living in villages and cities on the islands of southeast Asia, seeking to make God's Word intelligible to a people who only poorly grasped its meaning in the national language. We experienced many ups and downs along the way. There were frustrations mingled with joy. There were some tears, though many more laughs. And, in between all the comings and goings and interactions and cooperations, there were many songs on the journey.

# Acknowledgements

There are several groups of people and many individuals who have my highest respect and deserve recognition for their part in this story:

Those who prayed for the Tabulahan people, and for us, and gave (often sacrificially) to make it possible—parents, siblings, friends, Wycliffe colleagues and especially those from our home church at the time, Spreydon Baptist.

Our colleagues in Indonesia and the Philippines who mentored us, prayed for us, and shared our joys and frustrations. You are too many to mention by name here, though quite a few of you will get a mention in the following pages. I praise God for every one of you.

The people of Tabulahan, who welcomed us into their homes and their lives, taught us their language and culture, were patient with our mistakes and generous with all they had. So many became dear friends. In particular, I would like to thank our co-workers: Mariones, Daud, Ando', Sone', Äto', Uja and Iyä, and the Tabulahan translation committee members and reviewers.

My family members. Just by being there alongside us, our children: Fraser, Isaac and Esther shared the journey, opening doors into others' lives while filling ours with joy. I thank the Lord for each of you and now also for your godly spouses: Rebecca, Chuana and Nick. And finally, I want to thank my darling wife Delwyn who persevered with me through it all and whose life is a beautiful song.

Together, we praise the Lord for bringing His Word to these people made in His image. May it all be to the praise of His glory.

# 1
# Stuck in the Mud

It was a gutsy wee vehicle—the day before it had pulled a bus out of a ditch! What a wonderful machine that Toyota Land Cruiser was, its 4.2-litre petrol engine powerfully driving all four wheels simultaneously in the right direction. They were doing so now. But, with none of them touching the ground, we were on a slow track to nowhere. The thick, damp atmosphere and a thousand night sounds reminded us, as if we needed reminding, that we were in the jungle and unlikely to get out of this mud hole any time soon. The ruts I had been so consciously avoiding had been made by tractor wheels, twice as deep as the Toyota's. And now, having slid sideways on a slick clay slope, we were bottomed out, wheels spinning uselessly in deep ditches of sloppy mud.

We were borrowing the car from colleagues who were hoping to sell it before they returned to the States. I was keen on buying it, but, as we were light on funds, our colleagues were willing to let us take it on approval. They might have thought twice if they could see it now. Or the last time we were wheel spinning, an hour before.

Back then, after futile attempts to find rocks, logs or branches to wedge under the wheels, and as the last of the day's light ebbed away, we were relieved to hear a tractor coming from the other direction. A local firm, engaged in hauling ebony logs out of the forest, had made this road for (and ruined it with) their tractors and trailers. The tractor driver was very helpful and pulled us out to a spot where there was passing room.

"How's the road up ahead?" I asked.

"Bad," he replied as he drove away in the near dark, and the dozen passengers on the trailer waved us their parting sympathy. I should have realised that by 'bad' he meant impassable.

Foolishly, I pressed on. We had only gone another hundred metres or so when we slid off the tops and into the same muddy predicament. I cut the engine and looked across at my wife. Delwyn's face reflected the tension that my own was betraying.

"We'll be here for the night," I said.

"I know."

"I don't want to be here for the night," Fraser said.

"Well, I'm sorry," Delwyn answered our three-year-old, "but we don't have much choice. We'll just have to make the best of it." He did. After telling us a story and eating a snack he settled down to sleep in the back. And, after a drink, four-month-old Isaac did the same. Their two parents in the front did not sleep quite so easily. At least we had thought to buy a couple of pillows that morning.

With that in mind we had pulled up at the market in the coastal town of Mamuju and promptly locked the keys in the Land Cruiser. I was not keen to put on a breaking and entering show for the general populace, so Delwyn took the boys for a wander and drew the curious crowd with her. It seemed to me the easiest way to get in would be through the triangular vent window. However, to open this required pushing a button in on the locking handle before turning it through 90°. "If only I could pull that button towards me through the rubber seal," I mused. I figured two flat head four-inch nails could be the answer. There was a hardware store across the road. The proprietor assured me that it would be cheaper to buy them by the kilo. I don't think he had ever sold such a measly quantity before. Anyway, those two 4-inch nails saved the day. And the two pillows tried their best to save the night.

At first light I went to look for water. We were running low and would be needing more soon, especially as Delwyn was breastfeeding. I could, and maybe should, have gone back the way we came, knowing the river was less than half an hour away. But I was also keen to see how bad the road was ahead, so I went along the hilltop through the forest and started down the other side until I at last came to a muddy trickle emptying into a muddier puddle. The water was opaque, but thinner than anything collected in the tractor ruts, and I figured it would do. A friend from our home church had supplied us and others with Katadyn filters. I had a small pump filter we had brought with us that would make the water drinkable. It took 20 minutes and several filter cleans to fill a couple of bottles, and I started back up the hill. I had noted several places on the way down that we would have trouble getting past, and now looking at them again I felt miserable. "What have I done bringing my family here into the middle of nowhere?" I thought. "Have five years of study and preparation been for nothing, if we can't even get to the place where we are about to begin our translation project?" It was as low a moment as I had ever felt in my life.

I got back to the car an hour and a half after I'd left and told Delwyn the bad news.

"Some guys passed on their way to market," she said. "I asked them if they knew when a tractor might come through. They didn't know and carried on."

I told her that it could be days. I had heard that tractors did not pass by every day, and we knew there had been one through the night before. We weighed up our two options:

1. Wait for a tractor to pull us out and then head back to the city the way we came.
2. Wait for a tractor to pull us out, leave the car at the side of the track and travel with the tractor to the depot at Salu Batu, before walking further inland to the Tabulahan area.

The second option was our preferred one but was dependent on a tractor coming within the next day, as this was just to be a short exploratory visit. Even so, the way we were feeling at that moment we could have easily taken option 1.

Just then three young men with packhorses came along the road to head to a market nearer the coast. We called out our greetings and asked them where they had come from.

"From Tabulahan."

"That's where we are trying to get to!" We explained that we wanted to learn their language and planned to live among them in the future. Delwyn was particularly happy to meet these men, the first Tabulahan speakers she had met, each of whom we later came to know. It was clear that they would not be able to shift the car any more than we could, but they did offer to take our bags down to the river where it would be a better place to wait for a tractor. We hastily got together any necessaries, hooked the bags onto a saddle and walked with the men along the track.

Just before we reached the river, we met a tractor and trailer coming the other way. We thanked the Lord. We also thanked our new friends and wished them well on their journey.

The tractor driver listened to our predicament and took us back to where our dark blue Toyota sat marooned in the middle of the road, not unlike a stranded whale on a sandbar. Before long he had dragged the car backwards to a place where he could get past. It seemed there were two officials from the company travelling in the party, as well as 20 other passengers on the trailer.

I made my request. "Can we please travel with you to Salu Batu and just leave the car here?"

"Oh no, that's no good. Your car would be interfered with if you do that. Better you follow us, and we pull you out each time you get stuck. Your car will be safe at the depot." I thanked them and got back into the driver's seat.

"I'll drive it. You move over to the passenger seat." It was one of the bosses from the firm. "And your wife and children must go on the tractor. Too dangerous back here."

We acquiesced. I moved over, Fraser was placed on a woman's knee on a makeshift seat next to the tractor driver and Delwyn on a similar one held onto Isaac with one hand and gripped the tractor roof with the other. Twenty passengers swung their gaze intermittently between the unusual passengers before them and the unusual one behind. Between stoppages the car progressed under its own steam. But there was often an unavoidable drop into the ruts, or a deep mudhole awaiting its prey, and the tow rope had to be reconnected again. Eight times the tractor pulled us out before we reached the bottom of the hill and emerged from the forest. Delwyn and the boys joined me once more in the car, and we went on ahead to Salu Batu, where the tractor and trailer caught up with us half an hour after our arrival.

That night under a mosquito net in the ebony firm's radio room we slept well, far better than the previous night in the car's non-reclining seats. The fact that we had already secured the hire of a packhorse for the next day, and that we were exhausted from three days travel in unfamiliar surroundings, no doubt acted as soporifics.

Next morning at 7:30 we set out, Fraser on the horse* with the bags, Isaac in a backpack. The horse owner, Ambe Tori, recommended that we carry our shoes for the first half hour or so as there were several small river crossings. Once these were behind us, our feet were reshod along most of the trail. Five hours later we stopped for lunch at a deeper river crossing and refastened dry shoes on the other side. They were not dry for long. After lunch it began to rain. Some of our wet weather gear was deep in the thoroughly wrapped and tied bags on the saddle. We rearranged fidgety children to try to balance their needs with optimum progress, sometimes Fraser on my back, Delwyn carrying Isaac. At one point Delwyn fell and bashed her knee on a rock, damaged the umbrella, but managed to protect the baby. By this time, we were all soaked through.

Half an hour later we could see a village on the far side of a fast-flowing river. I remembered that our destination was just an hour past this last of the Makki-speaking villages before we reached the main body of the Tabulahan area. When I had come through here on a survey trip three months before, we had boulder-hopped across. Now, most of the boulders were covered and the river flow was a lot faster.

Delwyn was already concerned about how cold the boys must have been. When she saw the river, she wondered how we would ever get across. Our guide informed us that there was a bridge upstream that we could use. He would have to wade across with the horse lower down. Delwyn's heart sank again when she saw that the bridge spanning 12 metres or so was just two bamboo poles for feet to walk on and a single bamboo pole as a handrail. In subsequent years we became very familiar and even comfortable with such bridges.

---

\* All of the horses in the area are technically ponies, but as neither Indonesian nor Tabulahan have a word to distinguish horses based on size, neither do we here.

A head peered from a doorway. "Rain," it stated without wasting words.

"Yes, rain," I replied. We passed a few more houses. Several faces looked out from a paneless window frame.

"Rain. Stop first. Come on in. You can go after the rain. Stop first."

We looked at each other, nodded and entered, leaving our soggy, broken umbrella at the foot of the ladder.

It was a large room, about five metres square, and dark, lightened only dimly by the three small windows in the three walls that gave onto the outside world. But it was immediately clear that the several faces at the front window were not the only ones present. There were a couple of other travellers, as evidenced by their bags and wet clothing, and about 30 local residents. I suppose they had little to do on such a wet day but look for indoor entertainment provided by new faces passing through.

"Where are you from?" It was one of the other travellers who opened the conversation.

"From New Zealand."

"Where are you going?" he continued.

"To Tabulahan."

"I also. I'm the head of Tabulahan village. When the rain stops, we'll travel together. You'll stay at my house when we get there." Thus, we first met the no-nonsense Papa Tahe'. Three months earlier Papa Tahe' had been absent on a business trip, and my colleagues and I had stayed at the home of the village secretary, Papa Oba.*

We were able to dry off a little, change the boys' wet shirts

---

* Adults are generally addressed or referred to with a teknonym, typically the name of their eldest child, so Ambe X/Papa X (father of X) or Indo X/Mama X (mother of X). If they have no child they will often be known as Pua' X or Tanta X (Uncle or Aunt of X).

and get out the buried raincoats. Our hostess graciously brought out some hot coffee for us, very warming and very welcome. The rain had eased an hour later as we set off again with a larger travel party.

By late afternoon Fraser had had enough of being in the backpack and was desperate to walk for a bit. That slowed us down, and some of our companions went on ahead. On a climb, after the last of the smaller river crossings, Fraser voiced a plea. "Tabulahan, where are you? We've been looking for you many days and we can't find you." But Tabulahan found us! Twenty minutes later some young men came from the village to meet us. One hoisted Fraser up onto his shoulders and carried him the rest of the way.

The next four days and five nights were a whirlwind of new experiences for the family: of washing clothes, bathing, and toileting in a public space; of taking part in community work projects; of meeting scores of new faces; of learning new phrases in yet another language. The highlight, and what helped Delwyn make up her mind about whether this was where we were meant to be, came at the end of a ladies' house meeting on our last evening. In a letter home Delwyn wrote:

> *Late in the afternoon, while it was still raining heavily, the ladies gathered (though there were also several men in attendance). They sang some beautiful Tabulahan songs, and the leader of the congregation gave a short word in the Tabulahan language. Robin gave info on who we were, why we were here and where we came from. I gave a little run down on our trip to get there and how the Lord watched over us in the bush. Then we sang a song which they clearly enjoyed, asking for another. They gave us gifts of food and assurances of prayers for the journey back to*

*Ujung Pandang.\* I think the deciding point for me came at the end of this meeting when they all surged forwards to shake our hands with many saying, "You will come back, won't you?"*

The walk out next day was a lot easier than on the way in. Our host and hostess were headed for the weekly market at Lakähäng, near Salu Batu, so we were able to put our bags on their packhorse. Mama Tahe' gave a running commentary of points of interest, like all the places where horses had fallen over the edge into the Bonehau River and drowned. A young man carried Fraser, while I carried Isaac, so we were able to keep a good pace. Although there had been a lot of rain over the last few days, leaving deep mud in places on the trail and one or two landslides, we remained dry until the last quarter of an hour when it bucketed down. But knowing we were so close to shelter, that didn't matter.

In Salu Batu we were told that there would not be another tractor coming through for a couple of days. That gave us opportunity to spend most of the next day in Lakähäng, a large, mixed-language village with many Tabulahan speakers. That night, after hearing some of my conversation with one of our Muslim hosts at the ebony firm depot, Fraser asked his mother what a Christian is. It was time for bed anyway, so Delwyn had a good talk with him as she put him to bed under the mosquito net in the radio room. Delwyn wrote:

*I talked about what it meant to be a Christian. He was*

---

\* The largest city in Sulawesi and fifth largest in Indonesia (pop. 2 million approx.), formerly called Makassar. It has now been renamed Makassar after 28 years being known as Ujung Pandang, during which time the majority of this account takes place.

> very attentive and interested and when I asked if he wanted to be one of 'Christ's ones' too, he said yes. So, in an ever so simple way I led him in a short prayer. It's a beginning, and even in the experiences we've had since then, we've seen his faith grow in its own way.

Next morning, we were told that the tractor would be at Keang, a few kilometres away, and we could link up with it there to tow us when needed. Two of the men from the firm were keen to get to Polewali, so we offered them a lift. We left our other hosts some items, thanked them and reached Keang by 8:00 a.m.

A bulldozer had been working on the jungle track on the Keang side of the hill. We were pleased to hear that and see some improvement for the first kilometre or so. Then we got stuck. The tractor and trailer ahead of us reversed. We hooked up my tow rope, but that snapped without us budging more than a few inches. The tractor driver then produced a chain with thick links and hooked that up. It moved us a little further before that too snapped. Twice. By this time the tractor was also stuck.

Someone went to fetch a bulldozer. Delwyn took Isaac and Fraser up around the corner to pray. Half an hour later the dozer tracked its way up the hill and with its thick winch cable towed us out, towed the tractor and trailer out and bulldozed that particularly bad section. As I rounded the corner in the car, Delwyn and the boys were all smiles and hallelujahs and resumed their seats. They got out again for the worst of the mud holes, but there were only two more places where we actually had to be towed.

With no rain the night before, the river level at Kumaka was low and we were able to cross without incident. I turned to Delwyn as we drove out the other side. "Well, shall we buy the car?"

## 2

# Steep Learning Curves

We bought the car. That old blue rattler was to take us on a number of memorable trips in the coming months and years—no two the same, but all eventful.

So, what led us to this point in 1988 where we were about to begin a long-term language analysis and translation project? In itself it had been a long journey. I had studied linguistics at the University of Canterbury where I first met Delwyn, who was studying music there. At the time I had no thought about missions or how linguistics could be of any use in it. But after we were married in 1982 and seeking the Lord as to how we might serve him, Bible translation was impressed on us.

We made enquiries to Wycliffe Bible Translators, took one of their exploratory courses and began evening Bible college courses. After moving to Auckland to complete our Bible college studies, we spent a year in further field linguistics courses through the Summer Institute of Linguistics, first in New Zealand and then in Australia. A few months later we had raised enough support to head overseas: first for a 14-week course in Papua New Guinea, loosely called 'Jungle Camp', then working in a support role in PNG while awaiting our visas for Indonesia. The first year in Indonesia was spent learning the national language, Bahasa Indonesia, some language survey work and then teaching at a state university. Several months later we had reached this point.

*Songs on the Journey*

Between that first exploratory trip as a family and our first nine-week stint of village living we had to wait for written permission to begin our project in Tabulahan. During those four months we were visited first by my parents and then by our missions pastor and his wife, Don and Elane McKenzie (no relation). And in between we were improving our ability in the national language and practising the little bit of Tabulahan we had learned in February. The official permission to begin the project came through on May 17th just before I left to attend a conference in the UK on assessing translation needs. I was particularly impressed on my return with the progress of Delwyn and Fraser. They had spent time with a Tabulahan family in Palu while I was away and picked up quite a bit more vocab which they were now flaunting at home, knowing I had no idea what they were saying.

A week later we flew from our rented home in Palu to Ujung Pandang to get supplies together, load up the Land Cruiser which we had left with friends, and set off. Although the drive to the end of the vehicular road could be accomplished in 10 to 14 hours, depending on road and weather conditions, there was a requirement to stop at regency level government offices to process paperwork. This always made for a two-day drive before any walking could begin. Knowing how bad the road had been last time, I purchased a spare set of wheels with mud tyres in order to replace the road tyres at Mamuju and leave the unused ones there at the house of our colleagues, the Strømmes.

At one of the three offices where we were to report in Polewali, some 290 kilometres from the village, I was surprised to meet Papa Oba, the village secretary from Tabulahan, on one of his four-monthly visits to the regency offices. His was the home I had stayed in when I first went to Tabulahan the previous December. We were pleased to have him travel with us back to the village, even if it meant waiting a day for him to conclude his business.

We reached Mamuju the next day at dusk and enjoyed a pleasant evening and good night's sleep at the Strømmes' house. Next morning after breakfast we changed the wheels for those with mud tires and set out, hoping this trip would be less eventful than the last time we went inland along the Kalukku river. I was generally pleased with the state of the road up to the river crossing at Kumaka where we stopped to check its depth. It was higher than for any of our previous crossings, so we took local advice and waited a couple of hours. "A horse was washed away here yesterday. It drowned," a bystander remarked, encouragingly.

At 4:00 p.m. the level was lower but still marginally high. "It will rain tonight," someone said. "Better to go now while it is still light. If it rains tonight, you won't get across for at least another day." I was still dubious about the car making it at the present depth but was persuaded by his argument. I waded in once again to check the maximum depth, and to scout for any unseen large boulders, while on the bank Delwyn waited in expectation with the boys and Papa Oba. It seemed possible. We all resumed our seats inside.

With the engine at high revs, the Land Cruiser entered the water in low 4WD and crawled over the large cobbles. The water level rose quickly to the door, to our ankles, up the seats, but we were still progressing through the strong current. Then we ran into a boulder. We were only about a third of the way across. Before I could move the car in any direction, the engine died. The car slewed sideways in the current and came to a stop against another boulder. A couple of the onlookers on the bank waded in to our assistance. Delwyn's face looked grave as she passed Isaac out through a window to one of these strangers. After Papa Oba, Delwyn and I had got out, Fraser clambered through a window into waiting arms. And we all got back to shore safely.

By this time there was quite a crowd gathered at the riverside, some returning home from their gardens, others from markets. I told these men that I had a long rope and asked if they would be willing to help pull the car out. Several nodded. I waded back to the car to fetch the 20-metre length of rope we habitually carried and tied it securely to the back end. A few minutes later these 20 or 30 able-bodied men, who had gathered at the riverside at just the right time to witness the spectacle, pulled the drowned car back to the riverbank. It was clear we would not be crossing that day.

Kumaka was not so much a village as a collection of five or six houses sprawled untidily on the south side of the river. In the largest of these we were given shelter for the night. There was no food available to buy anywhere and the little we had we gave to the boys. That night the promised rain never came, and I wished I had not heeded the advice to try a crossing.

In the morning the water level had dropped considerably and returned to the usual flow. I dried off all the electricals and managed to get the engine started. It seemed gutless though and on three more attempts to cross, it had no power to even reach halfway. The only thing to do was to leave it at the riverside and walk the extra distance.

Someone who lived in Lakähäng told us that horses could be sent from there to get our stuff the next day. Armed with that assurance, we left a pile of bags in the care of the last night's host. I locked the car, covered it in a tarpaulin and tied it securely with rope. It was about 1:00 p.m. when we set out, fording the river and climbing the hill into the forest. We had some water with us and a little trail mix but had not eaten since breakfast the day before. Delwyn carried a small backpack with our camera, tape recorder, a couple of sarongs and a couple of nappies. Papa Oba had his own bag. I carried Isaac, and stout-hearted Fraser (almost four) was happy to walk. It was a very hot, sunny day. Once through the forest there was no cover, and by late afternoon I was feeling dehydrated and exhausted. Delwyn took Isaac and I took the backpack, and Fraser just kept on walking, encouraging his parents with made-up stories, just as we had done for him earlier in the day. It was getting dark by the time we reached Lakähäng. I was so exhausted that I couldn't eat a thing until I had slept for an hour.

Next day we heard that there was to be a wedding in Tabulahan the following day and that no one would be available to take horses to retrieve our baggage until the day after. "One day more won't hurt us," we thought naively. We walked a partly different route which was meant to be a shortcut, but turned out longer timewise, due to kilometres of knee-deep mud. Mud-wise, it was the worst trail either of us had ever been on and was probably as bad as it ever got on many subsequent journeys. I have vivid memories of hoisting Fraser up by one hand through many short sections, while Isaac, high and dry, surveyed the scene from his perch on my back. All in all, Fraser must have walked 25 of the 27 kilometres in that 24-hour period. We arrived a muddy bunch but very happy to finally be on familiar ground, and able to wash off in the river we already knew, that was to be our (and everyone else's) laundry and bathroom for the next nine weeks.

Again, we were given the small double bed just inside Papa Tahe's house. The rest of the room contained a dining table and benches and a small side table. Most nights we had the sole use of this room, our host family sleeping in the tiny bedroom and on mats in the kitchen. Occasionally other visitors slept on a mat next to our bed. We found the best sleeping arrangement was to lay Isaac between Delwyn and the wall and Fraser transverse at the foot of the bed. A thickish mosquito net gave a semblance of privacy.

A new morning broke: a beautiful golden light through silhouette coconut palms, not so common at this altitude. It felt great to finally be here, ready to launch into a new project: to learn the language, to help the community find the best way to write it down, to study the complexities of its grammar, to discover the key points of the culture and the best cultural equivalents in translating God's Word for a people still without it in their heart language. It was a special day, and how appropriate to begin with a wedding. We were invited along with the rest of the community, but what to wear? We had yesterday's rinsed, muddy clothing and the sarongs we had just slept in. Mama Tahe' told us sarongs would not be appropriate for a wedding.

"Could we borrow some clothes?"

"Really? You want to borrow clothes off us?"

"Yes, we have nothing else to wear. All our clothes are at Kumaka."

I think Mama Tahe' was secretly pleased that everyone would know Delwyn was wearing one of her outfits: a floral pleated skirt with polkadot top. I was equally resplendent in a borrowed lime green t-shirt the front of which read: 'THE BEST YEAR – editor's beat – IMPORTS – mysterious is in dream of ds of Rora and in the forest are friend'.

After six days some horses pulled up at the household of Papa and Mama Tahe'. They were carrying our bags. It felt like Christmas in July. Finally, we could wear some of our own clothes, clad the baby in nappies instead of small hand towels and, best of all, give our hosts the food items and other gifts we had brought for them. A small crowd watched us unpacking our stuff. Several items we placed on the side table next to the bed—things like a flashlight, pen, paper, books, soap, shampoo, comb and toothbrushes. These were all picked up and examined by curious hands and eyes, and most, in the weeks to come, borrowed. Items were always returned, but often not before we next needed them.

We had been hoping to take an SSB radio with us, but there was none available at the time of our departure from the city. The problem was that there were not enough licences for each team* to have a radio in the village, so teams had to bring their radio back to town so that someone else could use it when they went out. Before we had set out from Ujung Pandang, Ron Snell, our director, mentioned that should a radio become available, he would bring it out sometime during our stay. One night at about nine o'clock someone woke us up.

"Papa Fraser, Papa Fraser, your brother is here to see you."

"My brother? Can't be."

"Yes, it is!"

I stumbled from bed, grabbed a flashlight and opened the front door. In my dozy state I could just make out three blurry figures on the ground below the steps.

"Well," Ron said, "if it's inconvenient for you, we'll just turn around and go back to Ujung Pandang."

I laughed and invited them in. With Ron, were Dick and Sandy McNeill and their baby, Jana, about the same age as Isaac. They'd brought the radio, our mail and a whole lot of laughs for a couple of days before they returned to their roles in the city.

The radio could not have come at a better time. As well as reporting at the regency level in Polewali, as we had on our way in, we were to report at the district level offices at Mambi.

---

* 'Team' refers to any singles, couple or group working in a particular language context: in our case, our family.

But since we did not pass that way either coming or going, I would have to walk the two days there and the two days back again each time we came. Now, with the radio available, I did not feel so bad about leaving Delwyn and the boys. Delwyn loves people contact and, even though there was plenty of that in the village, she needed to speak English sometimes. With the radio we were able to have a short sked with colleagues in other parts of the island three times a week. From a kind man at the other end of the village I borrowed a couple of long bamboo poles about four inches thick at the base. These we planted some 20 metres apart to support the radio antenna. After checking that the small car battery and radio functioned, Ron and the McNeills headed back to Ujung Pandang.

On the day I set out for Mambi to report our presence, there was a group of folk from Tabulahan heading there too. I was pleased to be able to tag along with them as I had never been on that trail before. Delwyn and the boys accompanied us to the edge of the village where we said our goodbyes. Fraser had a pained expression, as if he might never see me again. That first day's walk led through patches of forest and cultivated land between two villages and then for several hours up forested ridges to Taora, a Bambam-speaking village, where most people from Tabulahan spent the night when travelling from either direction. Someone in our party had relatives living in a small village down the hill from Taora towards our destination, so this time we spent the night there. I shared a mat on the floor with six or seven young men. We were tightly packed like so many sardines in a bid to fit us all on the mat and to add more warmth than our thin sarongs would provide. I spent a good deal of the night wishing that I had been on the end as my two neighbours lay on the edges of my sarong, straight-jacketing me from any movement.

Next day we walked on mostly flat ground with several

river crossings until we reached Mambi on the far bank of a wider river. Government offices were closed by the time we reached there, so my reporting would have to wait for the morrow.

Next morning I met the district head and was reprimanded for not reporting the last time we had been in the area. I explained that we were only there for five nights that time and there was therefore insufficient time to spend four days coming to report. That was not a good enough reason, apparently. From now on, I was told, we must always travel through Mambi so we could report on the way into the village area. This would mean that the whole family would have a two-day walk in and out on the southerly route, instead of the expected one-day walk on the northerly route. I had much to ponder as I set out on my return from Mambi.

It was pleasant travelling alone that day on what was a broad and well-marked trail. Most of the journey was through the villages of Aralle, a dialect of the language we had come to study. It felt good to be able to call out greetings in their own language to folk at the roadside, in their fields or outside their mosques. They all answered happily, though with surprised expressions. After climbing the last hill, I bathed in a freezing stream and spent a pleasantly cool night in Taora. The following morning, I set out early and asked a couple of other earlybirds to direct me out of the village onto the right trail for Tabulahan. It was a clear morning, but I could see cloud below me obscuring the forest canopy. I hoped I wouldn't take a wrong trail before I reached the next village. After three hours of walking without seeing another soul, I was beginning to think that maybe I had taken a wrong turn. Half an hour later I came to the bottom of a ridge, the forest gave way to open cultivated land and I breathed a sigh of relief, knowing I was halfway there.

It was so good to be reunited as a family. Delwyn shared some encouragements she had received from the Word while I had been away: *"He gently leads those that have young"* (Isaiah 40:11). *"Not one will lack her mate…"* (Isaiah 34:16). (In my absence others had been able to fill in with some of the domestic tasks that I normally did.) And *"Grain must be ground to make bread; so one does not go on threshing it forever"* (Isaiah 28:28). This, she felt, was a promise that God would get us through the grind of language learning and eventually these people would get the Bread we were there to bring.

After a lovely family bathe up at the river mid-afternoon (culminating in a snake swimming over to us and being rapidly despatched), I heard that it was the 40$^{th}$ day since the son-in-law of the area's only church minister* had died. I had met him the previous December when he gave Ron, Rich and I a tour of Langsa' and some of the hamlets of Salu Leäng. I knew that the 40$^{th}$ night was a significant one for people there, and that there would be a remembrance service for the deceased up the hill. After walking 18 kilometres already that day, I could do without another three-kilometre hill climb. But I felt it was important to attend. Delwyn and the boys stayed behind because it had started raining. I don't remember much of the meeting, but I'm sure it was another piece in firming ties with a family that was later to become very dear to us. I got back down to Tabulahan about 9:30 p.m., leaving the folk up the hill surprised that I wasn't going to sleep there that night.

Our health had generally been good during this first village

---

\* At that time there was only one ordained minister for all the congregations of the area. He was generally referred to as *Pa' Pandita* (from Indonesian *Bapak Pendeta*), but he could also be referred to as *Ambe Datu* (Datu's father). We addressed him as *Pua'* (uncle).

living time, but our eldest had a long battle with a gut problem. He was off his food and kept losing weight. As the village toilet was a rock to squat behind in the river, and the river was a four-minute walk away, meeting his needs at that time became an almost constant traversing of that particular trail. We tried a number of remedies and all the usual worm treatments, and of course kept his liquids up, but nothing seemed to fix it. As the weeks went by, he became thinner and thinner. We had a stronger worm treatment with us that we had never used before which apparently would also deal with hookworm. We tried that and from that point he started putting weight back on, praise the Lord. That eased our anxiety level and helped us concentrate on language learning.

\*\*\*\*

We had now been in the country for 18 months. The first six of those had been spent in Palu, Central Sulawesi, where we lived with an Indonesian family. We ate all our meals together. This gave us three times a day when we could practice with family members the national language that we had been learning in our self-study sessions. Each afternoon we would also go for a walk around the neighbourhood, engaging anyone we could find in a chat to gain further practice.

After that we rented a house there as a base for all our comings and goings. Rentals were never on a weekly or monthly basis. It was even difficult to find a lease for only one year, payable in advance. The contract for the house we ended up leasing was for three years, payable in advance. Fortunately, rental prices were cheap by New Zealand standards, and we had just enough to cover it. Rent was also to be paid in cash back then. I went to the bank hoping to be able to get the full amount in Rp. 10,000 notes, the largest denomination at that time (roughly = NZ$10). The bank had run out of these. I feared that I might need a suitcase. At least they had Rp. 5,000 notes, so it could have been worse, but it still seemed like a huge number of wads I handed over to the landlord that morning.

The next couple of months were spent improving our ability in the national language and setting up the house with a few items of furniture and kitchenware, etc. I was also involved in a couple of sociolinguistic surveys in two parts of Central Sulawesi to determine things like where language boundaries lay, how closely related neighbouring dialects might be to each other, how vigorous was language use and whether it had been compromised by other groups moving into the area. This all helped form decisions as to priorities for language projects to be undertaken.

The first of the surveys that I was involved in was to determine the locations of the Tajio language population, whether there were dialects within the population, and how closely related it was to neighbouring languages. Four of us set out in the group van, planning to take wordlists for later comparison at several villages along the east coast of the isthmus north of Palu, before doing the same along the west coast. On the third day we met a line of trucks at a village right on the equator. A bulldozer had become utterly stuck in a mudhole in the main street, part of the trans-Sulawesi highway. It had been stuck for more than a day and no one was getting past. So, we postponed that part of the survey and instead returned to Palu, switched to motorcycles and focused on the west coast. Motorbikes were a good idea as there were several small river crossings and narrow trails to inland villages. The first of these river crossings showed me why my new shoes had only cost five dollars in the market—they had been assembled with water-soluble glue! As I was new to motorcycles, borrowing one for the occasion, I was the only one without bags on the rear of the seat. It was therefore up to me to take any pillion passenger when the need arose. So it was that I tried my best to keep upright on more than one muddy trail while carrying a village head or an imam who was to introduce us to the next village. I was not always successful in this.

A few days later two of us tried the east coast again, hoping that motorcycles would enable us to get past the blockage. At the same point we again encountered a sea of mud. Trucks were now negotiating front gardens in order to bypass the bulldozer. As we pushed our motorbikes with assistance through gardens knee deep in mud, we passed the said 'dozer. All that was visible was the roof of the cab at a level with the road, a square white island in a sea of brown. On our return, after completing the survey two or three days later, it had disappeared completely. The survey had given us some idea of the rather fragmented language situation along the isthmus, which had led to strong bilingualism in the area. Our conclusion was that this should not be a priority for a language project.

The next survey took three of us on foot through the Napu-Bada valley to survey the Sedoa, Napu, Besoa and Bada languages, returning by MAF plane to Palu. These languages were later worked on by colleagues. I was still wondering where we would end up.

As part of our agreement with the government, we took turns lecturing at universities in English language and/or linguistics. I was scheduled to be teaching syntax and phonology during the last semester of that first year, using Indonesian as the medium of instruction, so that gave me a real push in becoming as fluent as possible beforehand. Our friends, Phil and Denise Campbell, graciously put us up at their place in Ujung Pandang for that time. It was during that stay that our second son, Isaac, was born. And in December I postponed lectures for a week to make a first exploratory trip to Tabulahan with Ron Snell and Rich Kirby.

\*\*\*\*

Now here we actually were, a few weeks into language learning once again but this time without the aid of books. Initially we recorded every new expression we heard in notebooks, writing in phonetic script. Some people knew the national language well enough to translate these expressions for us, or to give us the Tabulahan equivalent of expressions that we were wanting to use. However, we had learned during training that better strides are made in language learning if a move to exclusive use of that language is made sooner rather than later. It might seem slower to begin with, but it will soon pick up pace and be more productive than using a *lingua franca* or go-between language. Also, it shows the native speakers that you are sincere in wanting to learn their language. And it will avoid either you or them lapsing into the national language whenever a difficulty in communication arises.

All good in theory. In practice Delwyn was a lot better at this than I was at the start. Delwyn would say as much as she could in Tabulahan, and wasn't bothered about throwing in the odd Indonesian word if necessary. I tried to be a linguistic purist. If I could say the entire sentence in Tabulahan, I would. But, if not, I would say the entire sentence in Indonesian. Of course, this had the adverse effect of encouraging my Tabulahan friends to use the national language along with me and I had lost an opportunity for local language practice. Sometimes I would hear Delwyn launch into a sentence in Tabulahan and I would think, "I know what she is trying to say, but she doesn't have half the vocab she needs to say that."

It didn't matter—her hearers also figured out what she was trying to say and gave her the rest of the sentence. Our host, Papa Tahe', loved to point out to me with a laugh that my wife spoke better Tabulahan than I did.

"How long have you been here?"

"Three weeks."

"Three weeks?" he laughed. "You'll never learn our language!"

Something had to be done. Delwyn and I made a pact that if either of us caught the other saying anything in Indonesian that we already knew the Tabulahan expression for, the culprit would have to make the next drink, or wash the nappies, or some other forfeit. It was a turning point for me and from then on I steadily used and learned more and more of the local language.

## 3

# A Dark Cloud

One morning in mid-August we awoke to the sound of a bamboo drum being beaten with a certain rhythm: tok, tok… tok; tok, tok… tok. We wondered what it meant. Mama Tahe' informed us that someone had died and sent one of her children to find out who it was. It was a woman in her forties who lived a few houses down from where we were staying. This was the first death in the community since we had started work there seven weeks before. In the years to come there were many more. We visited the household of the bereaved along with many others from the village, each household taking gifts like rice, sugar, kerosene, etc. The body was lying on a sarong and draped with a sheet. Outside, men were busy hollowing out a kapok log for a coffin, while women decorated a plank lid for it with ribbon and R.I.P.-type expressions in Indonesian. Others were chopping firewood and butchering a pig to feed guests. The funeral would be held the following day, by which time family members from further afield could be summoned.

Early next morning Delwyn and I went to the outbuilding where the SSB radio was kept. Ron's voice came up first with an important announcement. Officials from the central government had determined that our organisation's current five-year contract, due to expire in 20 months' time, would not be renewed thereafter. It felt like a heavy body blow.

Exactly fifty days ago we launched this language project full of hope and began by celebrating a wedding. Today, hearts heavy with the implications of not being able to continue beyond a year and a half, we would be attending a funeral. The day's sunshine belied the mood of our hearts.

Next morning down at the river the Lord gave Delwyn an encouraging song: "I will praise you Lord, although I don't know why things are happening as they are… Your thoughts are not my thoughts and Your ways are not mine, but I know what you have planned to do will come to pass."\*

That afternoon on our daily walk to visit one or two households we had not yet visited, Delwyn and I discussed what the news might mean for our work there. Perhaps we should spend the rest of the next year and a half helping another translation team who were already further along in their work. Maybe we could home-school kids for one or more families, freeing up the teacher to be working on translation.

We asked Don and Shari Barr, pioneers of the Central Sulawesi work, that question the next time we saw them. We would have loved to help them and other Palu-based families in any way we could.

"No, you carry on what you are doing," Don said. "Learn as much as you can during these next 18 months. You never know how the Lord might open up some way to continue beyond that time."

He did. Twice the government allowed SIL a short six-month extension beyond the non-renewed five years. Twice we pushed back our home assignment to make the most of that extended time. In the end it meant we had been away from New Zealand for four years and four months, but we had spent a good two and a half years of that getting to grips

---

\* See song: 'Although I Don't Know Why'

with the Tabulahan language. And when we finally did head home for a break, we were fluent in general conversation and had even begun translating portions of the Word.

But that was more than two years away. Right now, we were coming to our last two weeks of this first nine-week stint in the village. We continued to observe and note down cultural norms—the way things were done around the village—and to record new vocabulary in our notebooks and oral texts on a tape recorder. However, the house in which we were staying had no clear space where we could work regularly. This would be exacerbated in future trips when we would be bringing a computer, books and other items to set up more permanently. Also, the lack of privacy was beginning to wear on us. I asked Papa Tahe' if there was a house that we would be able to rent in the village. He said that there was none.

On one of our trips up to Salu Leäng to visit Ambe Datu I explained to him what was on my mind. The minister was a quiet-spoken man with a lot of wisdom. He told us that it would be inappropriate for us to move house within the village, as that might be seen as a slight on our host.

"However," he continued, "if you were to move villages, then of course you would have to move house."

"Is there a house in Salu Leäng we would be able to rent?" I asked.

"No, but you could live here with us. My house is bigger. You would have room to work."

This was true. Still, I was concerned that, as he was an important figure in the area, there would be a lot of comings and goings and meetings that would potentially disturb whatever set-up we had. The front half of his house was a more modern construction than the traditional rear portion and was two metres above the ground.

"Could we live under the front of the house?" I asked.

"Not a good place. The ground is damp down there and it is next to the chicken coop."

I explained that I would put down a tarpaulin on the dirt and put up some bamboo walls to keep the animals out. He must have thought us a little weird, but he conceded that it was a big enough area and would give us semi-independence if that was how we wanted to live. It was settled. This was where we were to make our home for the coming times in the village area.

With that positive silver lining in the dark cloud of uncertainty hanging over the future, we prepared for the journey out. On our last day Delwyn wrote:

*I've been sitting here stewing while Isaac is sleeping, giving a lot of thought, and I admit worry, for the trip tomorrow. I wish it was over and we had reached Le'beng. I've been reading some good scriptures to renew my strength and to try to make the sinking feeling of all the possible things that could go wrong on the road subside. Among them was "The joy of the Lord is your strength." And the context of that was that the people were responding to hearing God's Word made meaningful to them, which I thought was very relevant.*

The trip to Salu Batu went remarkably smoothly, despite the mud. Fraser was able to ride with the bags after the horse caught up with us two hours along the trail. A tractor was due to be leaving Salu Batu at about 3:45 p.m., heading for a depot near Le'beng, and we would be able to get a lift with it to the river crossing at Kumaka. The road had been worked on and was much improved. And crossing the river on the tractor and trailer, instead of wading or driving through on smaller wheels, kept us high and dry when we arrived at about 5:00 p.m.

## A Dark Cloud

The tractor driver, a kind man named Randu, was amazing. He was happy to wait for us while I tried to get the Land Cruiser going. Straight away we could see that things were amiss. The ropes securing the tarpaulin had been taken, though not the tarpaulin itself, strangely. There was a keyed lock on the hood that had been broken open, though the disconnected battery was still there. All of the tyres had been deflated. Once we had reconnected the battery and inflated the tyres with a hand pump, I tried to start her up. There was still spark in the battery, but no way would it start. Randu said he would use the tractor to try tow-starting it. As soon as he pulled us backwards to the roadway it was clear that no wheels were turning. The brake shoes had seized on the drums.

While this was going on, Delwyn was chatting with local folk and watching us getting nowhere. She began to fear that we would be stuck here for a week while we waited for a mechanic to come from Mamuju. Another stranded motorist was sitting on his 4WD. He told her that his car had drowned in the river three weeks before and he had been waiting all that time for a mechanic to come from the coast. Her heart fell further. Not only was a further delay not a happy thought, Delwyn was keen to get back to town soon as Isaac had a high temperature. Randu and the other driver set about taking off the wheels and hammering the drums to free up the brake shoes. Finally, we could try tow-starting the car. No go. Something was clearly wrong with the engine, but none of us knew what. And one other thing we had discovered during the towing: the car had no brakes whatsoever.

By now it was dark and Randu said he had to get going. I asked if he would be willing to tow us to where we might get help. He was reluctant, especially as the car was without brakes and there were inclines along the road. In the end he agreed provided that we use a log along with the tow rope to keep from bashing into his trailer. We found one that looked like it might suffice and which, after snapping twice in the first couple of kilometres, held strong thereafter. It was a winding road and dark without headlights. To use them would have quickly flattened the battery. A traveller from the trailer sat next to me holding a flashlight out of the window and trying to keep the beam on the tow rope while I steered. I was glad Delwyn and the boys were praying up in the tractor cab.

We reached the ebony firm's depot about three hours later. Here Randu swapped the tractor for a car and drove us the four kilometres to Le'beng. We had never stayed in Le'beng before, but Mama Tahe' had a relative living there whom she said would look after us. Mama Eda was gracious enough to do so. Not many people would welcome complete strangers into their home at 11 o'clock at night!

We were exhausted, but it was a disturbed night's sleep with Isaac feverish. In a letter home Delwyn wrote:

*I woke so glad to not be still at Kumaka, but I had this awful feeling that we would be here for a long time. I wondered what parts of the car would need to be fixed, and I was also worried about Isaac who was still running a temperature and not happy in himself.*

*I went out to wash the clothes—it was wonderful because they had a well with a hand pump right by the house! When I came back, Robin had wandered off with the kids for a walk and the house was empty. I took the opportunity to do my reading for the day and I was looking for some encouragement. Needless to say, I was a little disappointed that the planned allotment for the day was Lamentations. Lamentations was just how I felt, but I didn't think it was what I needed right then. Anyway, I started reading and got to where it said: 'I remember my affliction and my* wandering… yet this I call to mind and therefore I have hope: Because of the Lord's great love we are not consumed, for His compassions never fail. They are new every morning; great is Your faithfulness. I say to myself, 'the Lord is my portion therefore I will wait for Him… Who can speak and have it happen if the Lord has not decreed it? Is it not from the mouth of the Lord Most High that both calamities and good things come?' Lam 3:19-24, 37-38

By the time I got further down the passage: 'Streams of tears flow from my eyes…' it was very relevant. Although I often sing the song that goes with the passage ('The Steadfast Love of the Lord'), this day it took on new meaning. It turned out very much to be a day of waiting too, just not knowing what was going to happen and whether we would ever get back to Ujung Pandang.

After breakfast I walked back up the road to where we had left the car the night before. I didn't see Randu, but there were a few other ebony firm employees milling around, including three men who were not qualified mechanics but who worked on keeping all the firm's vehicles operating. I asked for their help in getting the Land Cruiser going. It seemed they did not have a lot of work on that day, so they agreed to see what they could do. I was unsure how I was going to pay for this work as funds were getting precariously low and there was still a journey of more than ten hours driving ahead of us. I spent the rest of the morning alternating between chatting with bystanders and local villagers who were wandering along the road, and checking on progress. On one of these checks I was relieved to hear the engine kick into life. A fourth man who was a qualified mechanic had arrived and lent his expertise. He explained to me that someone had changed cables around, so it was no wonder the engine refused to start the day before.

They were about to set to work on the inoperable brakes and told me to come back in another couple of hours.

While I was waiting, I heard some yelling and saw some men running into the forest behind the depot. "What's the excitement?" I asked one of the tail-enders.

"Python!" he exclaimed. "Big one." I had read that reticulated pythons could grow to 30 feet in length and the skin of large ones could command a good price, hence all the interest. I joined him in running after the others. Before we had gone 100 metres, the group came running back.

"Not a python," one said in answer to my query.

"Not a python?"

"No, a big snake, but not a python."

I didn't get to see it but concluded from their description that it was most likely a king cobra, the second largest kind of snake there.

It was 2:30 in the afternoon when I returned to the mechanics. They had got the brakes bled and functioning but had no more brake fluid to fix the clutch. Apparently, it would still work if I pumped it a few times. I thought of the Rp. 20,000 I had in my pocket, hoping it might cover costs.

"How much do I owe you?" I asked the one on the left.

"I don't know. Ask him."

"Don't ask me," said the second. "Ask him."

I asked the third. "It's up to you," he told me. "Just cigarette money."

"Well, I want Rp. 5,000," the expert latecomer put in bluntly. I spotted Randu and wanted to give him Rp. 5,000 also. That left me with only Rp. 10,000 to spare. I asked the other three if they would mind sharing this small amount, equivalent to not much more than three dollars each. They seemed very happy with that. We thanked each other and I drove back to Le'beng.

Meanwhile Delwyn felt the Lord's nudge that she should

## A Dark Cloud

get herself and the boys bathed, and all the clothes packed up. It was beginning to rain as I pulled up outside Mama Eda's house. I left the engine running because the battery had been somewhat drained. Mama Eda wanted me to come in and eat before we left, but I was keen to get moving because the Lombang-Lombang River could flood if it rained heavily, and I would need to get the clutch seen to at Mamuju before the long drive to Ujung Pandang the next day.

It was an amazing feeling as we drove away—not only having our previously drowned car more or less functioning, but having the family together and in our own private space, something we had not experienced for nine weeks. Each time I needed to change gears I had to pump the clutch 20 or 30 times to build up enough pressure, so I drove for the next hour and a half in second and third to avoid too many gear changes on the way to Mamuju.

On the off chance that someone might have been able to pick it up for us and bring it into the village during our stay, we were expecting some mail to have been redirected to the post office box of our friends the Strømmes, whose house we had overnighted in nine weeks before. They were away in a village up the coast now, so we would have to look for other accommodation. But we were still hoping to access our mail that evening if at all possible. It was a long shot, calling at the post office after dark, but we were keen to get news from home. After finding a cheap hotel and getting something to eat, we headed for the post office. As expected, it was closed and locked, but there was a light on inside. I knocked and a man holding a paint brush came to the door dressed only in his underwear. He stated the obvious. "The post office is closed for the day. I'm just doing some painting."

"We were hoping to pick up some mail sent here for us, care of Strømme's mailbox."

"Oh, if that's all, no problem. Come in and find it."

He returned to his painting, and we located the mailbox and took out the package addressed to us. Inside were a few letters, and, sent to the boys from their grandmother, that wonderful book: *Green Eggs and Ham*. Dr Seuss was always a favourite. How blessed we felt. Food to eat, a roof for the night, news from home and something new to read to the boys before bed. We returned to the hotel a happy bunch.

An hour earlier when we had located the hotel, a slightly grubby place along the waterfront, the proprietor at first said that they had no rooms. But when pressed, he conceded that they did have one very small room (about seven feet by five feet) with just a double bed. "Too small for you all," he said. We assured him that it was just what we were used to. I don't think he believed us.

# 4

# New Trail, New Village, New Home

"May I leave my child with you?" I asked the bewildered old man. "I need to go back down the trail to help my wife and my other child." The ancient villager sat cross-legged on the floor of his house, a small kerosene lamp scattering a dim arc of light across the room. "It will only be half an hour or so," I explained.

Surprise continued to register on his weathered face, but he answered kindly. "Yes, of course you may."

I thanked him, handed Isaac over, and his wrinkled brown hands held our little, white one-year-old with all the care of a grandfather. I ran back down the hill as the darkness of nightfall intensified.

Two days earlier we had set out from Ujung Pandang on this, our second nine-week period of living in the Tabulahan area. This journey would be different—it would be the first time we went in via the southerly route, meaning we would be able to report at government offices in Mambi, as requested. We spent the first night in Polewali in order to report the next day at government offices there as usual, and to change the wheels to ones with mud tyres. (We had taken these to Mamuju last trip, but brought them to Polewali on the way back, so as to use them in future on the Mambi road.) Papa Abri, the son of our soon-to-be new village host, had a house in Polewali and was willing to store our spare wheels and put us up when we passed through.

## Songs on the Journey

At Papa Abri's house we met Gerson, a young Tabulahan man who lived in Mambi. He was keen to get a lift back home and we were able to help him with this. The road up to Mala'bo' was winding and hilly but paved and posed no problems. In contrast, the 28 kilometres from Mala'bo' to Mambi was unpaved and varied between patches of smooth, hard sand, rock, baked clay and mud. At least the ruts were only the same depth as the Toyota's new mud tyres. There was one gully spanned by narrow logs—three for each side's wheels—which was a little precarious, necessitating the evacuation of all passengers. But, apart from this, I didn't find the road too bad on this first occasion. Delwyn thought otherwise. I knew she never liked that road, but it was not until reading her journals lately that I discovered how intensely.

> *Robin was reasonably happy with the road, so I tried to keep my sheer terror to myself and trust the Lord. Feeble attempts at the song, 'Shepherd of my soul, I give you full control, wherever You may lead I will follow...' were a test of trust, so different to singing it in a comfy room on a Sunday night! Fraser, sitting in the back merrily eating a salak, asked, "Daddy do you think the road to Mambi is a good road or not?" in the kind of voice that one would use in choosing which T-shirt to wear for the morning. I could hardly believe my ears. Even as he was saying it we were bouncing around the ruts and ditches like a boat on rough seas!*

We stayed the night in the household of Mama Rudi, Gerson's mother. Gerson arranged three packhorses for the next day, along with three of his friends to guide them. I knew the trail that first day was mostly level until a steep hill climb at the end, but it was 26 kilometres and with several river

## New Trail, New Village, New Home

crossings, so we were hoping to leave early to avoid the worst of the day's heat. While we waited for horses, I went to the district offices to report our presence and projected time frame in the area. By the time the horses were rounded up, fed and saddled, and our bags tied in place, it was 10:00 a.m. Fraser walked for some of the journey, but rode at times. At one gully he tumbled backwards over the horse's rump, almost ending up in the water as his mount jumped out of the stream and up onto the bank. By mid-afternoon the horses and their handlers had gone on ahead and Fraser no longer had opportunity to ride, even though tired.

It was late in the afternoon by the time we crossed the long bamboo bridge near Sodangan and began the climb. The higher we climbed, the slower our progress. In the end, with rain coming down and night fast approaching, we were quite exhausted. I suggested that I go on ahead, leave Isaac in Taora and come back to carry Fraser. So it was that, at the first house in Taora I reached, I surprised an old man I had never met with a plea to baby-sit.

Back down the trail I was relieved to find the other two still plodding ever onwards and upwards, though Fraser had been in some distress at how long I had taken. The sky was now pitch black. Before long we had made it the rest of the way up the hill to the village. At Taora the old man explained that the rest of his household had gone to a house meeting, but he was too tired. He apologised that he was unable to provide a drink for us. Delwyn stayed and chatted with him for a bit while I ferried the boys to Mama Semeng's house with the aid of a borrowed lantern. The horses and their handlers had already been there some time.

Mama Semeng was the world's most hospitable woman. She taught at the intermediate school at Taora which meant that she lived there during term time. During the holidays she would return home to Tabulahan to be reunited with her husband and her four boys. But whether she was in Taora or not, she made her home there available to Tabulahan folk (and others like us) passing through. We have seen her small house packed with travellers, all of whom she fed and bedded down for the night before sending them on their way the next day.

We were still recovering next morning, and Mama Semeng recommended that we spend an extra day in Taora to regain our strength before we tried walking another day on a worse trail. That, coupled with the fact that our horse handlers did not want to go further than Taora, helped us make that decision. This would mean either finding other packhorses or porters in Taora, or leaving our baggage there and sending men with horses back from Tabulahan area to pick it up. As it happened, we had to do both. No one in Taora had horses, but we did find five young men happily ready to carry Fraser and some of our baggage.

Although a very up and down trail, the first part of that second day's walk was always something special, hiking through lush rainforest for three hours. Beyond that, the easier terrain through pockets of cultivated land and scrubby regrowth was generally hotter unless it was raining, with little shade from the sun's glare. This day the weather remained fine and hot throughout the walk until we arrived mid-afternoon. The last three kilometres from Tabulahan to Ambe Datu's house at Salu Leäng was uphill. For those of us not used to walking long hikes in tropical heat it was taxing. For our porters it was nothing and, after a drink and being paid, they trotted off down the path to head straight back to Taora in the rain that was just beginning to fall.

Salu Leäng is not so much a single village like Tabulahan, but more of a series of hamlets. Once the Ma'bu River is crossed at an area known as Pikung, a steep climb leads to

Panampo where there is a church surrounded by a sizeable group of houses. From there the track curves around rice fields to Palempäng, Sohongang, Kahangang and Bulung, each of which are small hamlets. After another rise to a flat-topped ridge there is an open area encircled with houses. This is Tamonseng, as large as Panampo. Across an adjacent ridge is Kombeng, where Salu Leäng's elementary school sits above another church and collection of houses. Further up above Tamonseng there is a larger church and several houses forming the hamlet of Pahihuang. This is where we were to live with the minister, Ambe Datu, whom everyone referred to as Pa' Pandita, and his family.

For the first two weeks until we had converted the sub-floor area of Pa' Pandita's house into a flat, we lived upstairs with him and the others in the household: Indo Datu, his wife; Mama Ondong, their recently widowed daughter; two or three of her five children, the others being away studying; Uja, an adopted nephew; and Lete, an adopted niece.

Pa' Pandita helped us find three men to cut bamboo, split it, flatten it and weave it into panels to form walls and two doors. The area we were to occupy was six metres by 5.5 metres (about 350 square feet) and it took the men just three days to complete this. I also had them make a couple of split bamboo roller blinds to cover the window openings at night to keep bats out. The floor was damp soil, so I covered it up with two plastic tarpaulins I had brought with us for that purpose.

In answer to my question as to what appropriate wages per day would be, our host informed us that we should give them the same amount that anyone might be paid for working a day in someone else's fields, namely Rp. 1,000 (at that time about one NZ dollar) and provide their midday meal and cigarettes.

At the risk of going against the cultural norm, I said, "I'm happy to provide them with the meal and the wages, but I really don't want to give them cigarettes. I would rather give them extra money that they can use for other things if they want to."

"But we always give our workers cigarettes."

"Cigarettes are bad for health," I said. "And I don't want to make anyone sick. My grandfather died young because he smoked a lot. I really don't want to buy cigarettes for anyone."

"Well, in that case, give me the extra money and I will buy cigarettes for them with it."

"No, that is not what I mean. If I give them extra money, they can use it for something else like food or clothing or children's schooling. If they want to use it to buy cigarettes, well, that is up to them."

Our host yielded to my stubbornness and foreign ways, and I gave each man a day and a half's wages for each day as well as their midday meal. They all brought their own cigarettes with them.

One of the men who had some carpentry skills spent an extra few days constructing some furniture. First was a three-metre-wide wooden sleeping platform, where the boys could sleep on one side under their mosquito net and Delwyn and I on the other side under ours. He then constructed three identical boxes with hinged lids, each measuring half a metre by half a metre by one and a half metres. Two of these were to be used as storage chests and double as seating at a table we had borrowed from upstairs. The third was to be a vertical storage cupboard with shelves added. All of these used rough-sawn timber, so they fitted in well with my own bush carpentry: a bamboo and plank kitchen counter, something similar as a writing desk, and a bamboo and rattan swinging couch suspended from the upper storey's floor joists.

By this time the remainder of our chattels had been retrieved from Taora by our friend Ambe Tori, whose equine services we had used in the past. These included a primus stove, a small tin box oven just big enough to perch on the stove, a pressure lantern, basic kitchenware, plastic jerry cans and filter candles for purifying water, a large aluminium basin for laundry and bathing the baby, and a couple of kapok mattresses. Our apartment was the Ritz.

During the day the two doors were often open. This led to a stream of chickens filing through the room, pecking at scraps and leaving deposits in payment. Sometimes it was dogs, but thankfully they were less generous. Coupled with that, there was a never-ending shower of crumbs emanating from floorboards and floor joists above us as thousands of boring insects chewed their way through their woody larder. Delwyn dusted down horizontal surfaces and swept the tarpaulin floor twice a day, but before long a certain grittiness held sway again.

During the evening we would light the kerosene pressure lamp for the meal, for clearing up and getting the boys to bed, then turn it off. This must have seemed like an extravagance to our neighbours who only ever used pressure lamps for gatherings. At other times we used the ubiquitous candle-type kerosene lamps, typically made from a small sardine can, with a length of old t-shirt inside a bit of umbrella-handle tubing for a wick. Whatever we were using for lighting, there were often sets of eyes three or four feet above the ground peering through the woven bamboo walls at the novelty we were.

Night visitors did not necessarily restrict themselves to looking in. The most common were the four-inch huntsman spiders that patrolled the walls looking for bugs. One of the men who made our walls said to us, "We don't kill them because they hold the roof on in a high wind. And they die with their legs hanging down, poor things." If we were late rolling down the blinds, we occasionally had a bat flying around the room and, once, inside the mosquito net. At floor level it was usually rats, toads or tree frogs. But one night, as we sat reading on the swinging couch, it was a black snake that slithered beneath us. We lifted our legs, glad that the couch was as legless as the snake. It found another gap in the opposite wall and continued on its way.

"Something just grabbed my toe!" I said to Delwyn one night after we had just got into bed.

"It was probably just my foot brushing against it."

"No, it grabbed my big toe!" I insisted, pulling back the sheet with one hand and reaching for the flashlight beneath the pillow with the other. "There!" There in the flashlight beam was a black rhinoceros beetle, the same size as and happily clinging to my big toe with his hooked legs.

"Must have come in with the sheets when I brought them in from drying today."

"That doesn't make him any more welcome," I said, and threw him out the window.

But mostly our visitors came during the day. And those that were people we did our best to make very welcome. We were wanting to practise all the language already learned and keep increasing our vocabulary and new structures, so it was a delight to have visitors come for whatever reason, just as it was to visit them in their houses. In addition to this we were looking forward to having regular paid language helpers come now that we were set up with workspace.

I realised that it would be difficult for the same person to come daily, as everyone had other work commitments with fields and crops to tend. But perhaps I might find four men who could each come one day a week. Delwyn was looking for a woman to come and assist her with language learning at least one day a week. We had learned that it is wise practice to ask your host to find people to work with. To this end, I asked Pa' Pandita for help in finding people who would be available and suitable as language helpers. He identified four men and one woman who would be appropriate. Delwyn had joked that there would be some toothless old fellow among them, and sure enough, one of the men had no teeth, but that didn't stop him being an excellent storyteller with good, clear diction despite gums devoid of ivory. He produced so many good texts for us to analyse and was always ready to be recorded on cassette tape, whether he was preaching, praying, explaining a process or just recounting a traditional yarn.

And his daughter turned out to be the most helpful person we encountered, especially during those early years. She faithfully came each Friday after finishing teaching to spend the afternoon with Delwyn, helping her in all aspects of language learning. She also helped us in recording conversations with other native speakers so that we could memorise them in order to establish sentence patterns. She was a local mover and shaker, such that if we needed to get a project off the ground, she would make sure the community got behind it. When it came time to begin translation of the Word, she was the one ready and willing to help us start. We felt the Lord had prepared her for this role (see inset).

\*\*\*\*

It was still more than a year and a half before we would begin any drafting of Scripture in the Tabulahan language, but things were beginning to fall into place for a good foundation. Each day there was progress on at least one area, whether data gathering, text glossing, adding new terms to a dictionary database, listening to pre-recorded conversations or just listening to others' conversation that we did not yet understand, but silently tracked the intonation patterns anyway as young babies do. For that, in a sense, is what we still were.

## The Two Mary Joneses*

Two hundred years ago a young Welsh girl by the name of Mary Jones heard that there were Welsh Bibles for sale. She longed for one of her own and after six years had finally accumulated enough money for one, so she set out to buy her Bible in a town 20 miles away. It took her all day to get there but on arrival she found that they had all been sold out. Moved by her deep desire for a Bible in her language, the minister whom she had travelled to see gave her his own personal Welsh Bible. Soon after, he returned to England and shared Mary's story with church leaders and businessmen. As a result, the group formed the British and Foreign Bible Society to aid the Bibleless peoples of the world.

About 80 years ago, a young man in Indonesia heard the story of Mary Jones, which had been translated into the national language. He decided that if he ever had a daughter, he would call her 'Mary Jones', or 'Mariones' as he heard it in Indonesian. His first-born was a girl and so indeed he named her Mariones. She grew up and became a respected school teacher in the area. In 1989 when we started working among Mariones' people to learn their language in order to translate God's Word, it was she who turned out to be our greatest help in those early days of adjusting to language and culture. With her help we were able among other things

---

\* There was arguably a third 'Mary Jones' involved in this story—the person most influential in my own conversion. Born Edna May (=Mary) Jones, she was my mother.

to record prepared conversations for language learning, start song writing, prepare a writing system for the language, learn much about local customs, and get a writing competition off the ground. When it came time to start translation, she was the only one ready and willing.

Before our first furlough she began translating the Joseph story from Genesis with Delwyn and portions of Mark's Gospel with Robin. While we were on furlough, she continued to draft Genesis and portions of Exodus. When first published, it was the first translation by our organisation of the whole of Genesis into any of the languages of the country. The consultant who checked it commented that it was an excellent translation, largely due to the good first draft done by Mariones.

Her father could not have known when he named her just how significant it would be that like the first Mary Jones who was instrumental in bringing the Bible to many without, so her namesake across the world and centuries later would become instrumental in bringing God's Word to her people in their own language.

## 5

# Christmas Guests

Christmas was approaching—our first Christmas in the Tabulahan area. While we were looking forward to the local celebrations we had heard about, we were also looking forward to having guests from the outside world share this very different Christmas with us. We were hoping to have two colleagues come to share in our Christmas, whatever that might mean in our new situation. Susan Shore, a fellow Kiwi, at that time worked in all manner of roles in Ujung Pandang; and Christine Varley, a teacher from Australia, was itinerating around Central Sulawesi to help translators with their children's education.

We had given the two young women a brief outline of how to get to Mambi, where I hoped to meet them on a given day. However, not all details were settled and there was a major problem in communicating. The car battery for the radio had gone flat and we were getting next to nothing in terms of solar charging, due to cloudy weather and surrounding trees. Accordingly, the radio was barely functioning. There was still enough charge to receive, but transmitting took more power. It seemed no one at the other end could hear much when we tried to transmit.

Two days later it was much the same, even after I hooked up eight D cells I had bought at the market. Apparently, the hearer at the other end was only able to get the first syllable we spoke before transmission cut out. Some communication was possible, but only by playing Twenty Questions. We were not able to say, 'how copy, over', 'roger', or even 'affirmative' or 'negative'. We could, however say, 'yes' or 'no' in answer to their questions.

So it was that, when it came time to confirm with Susan and Christine details of their arrival and where they should avoid getting off public transport, we had to rely on them asking us the right questions. After getting off a bus from Ujung Pandang, we were hoping they would get a vehicle from Polewali straight through to Mambi, and not get a Mamasa vehicle which would drop them off at Mala'bo'. The problem with Mala'bo' was that vehicles passing through there on their way to Mambi were invariably full. Unfortunately, they did get a Mamasa vehicle, spent the night in Mamasa and next day returned to wait in Mala'bo'. They waited all day and all night.

I arrived in Mambi after the two-day walk from Salu Leäng, surprised that they had not already arrived. I watched for vehicles coming into town and asked every driver if he had seen two European women. At midnight a vehicle reached Mambi and the driver said that yes, he had seen them at Mala'bo'. Now Delwyn had expressly forbidden me to "drive on that awful road to Mala'bo'." I think she had visions of the car falling off the thin logs over the gully. There is a time for wilful disobedience. This was such a time. One of our colleagues once described Mala'bo' as "the armpit of Sulawesi." Whether or not that was true, Susan and Christine were relieved not to be stuck there another night when I picked them up. We arrived safely at Mambi at midday, had a meal and rested. It was too late to start walking that day.

The next two days were the usual slog, with Susan finding it particularly hard going, especially as the porter had walked on ahead with her drinking water and the shoes she had taken off for a river crossing. She arrived exhausted and with very sore feet. At Taora Papa Semeng was there, and Mama Semeng put us up with her usual care. Susan later wrote in a newsletter:

*The man of the house said that he felt really sad when he saw me arrive, I was so exhausted. It was an hour before I was able to do anything else but sit and drink the strong black coffee we were served... I really praise God for the hospitality extended to us by the Indonesian people, and their willingness to take strangers into their homes to spend the night or just to give us a drink along the way.*

It was a happy reunion when we finally made it to Salu Leäng. Delwyn and the boys had been alternating praying and wondering with waiting and worrying for the extra day or two of our delayed arrival. Susan was too sore to make it up the hill to Salu Leäng that day, so stayed in Tabulahan with Papa and Mama Tahe'. Next day we went down to accompany her up to our place. Our flat was on the small side for accommodating guests, but the house upstairs had a spare room for Susan and Christine to sleep in. They spent the days with us, and we had our meals together in our tiny kitchen.

For the week leading up to Christmas, each church congregation has something going on each evening. Often this is a special service for some group or other within the congregation, such as the young people's, or the women's group. Such services frequently feature a 'Shining Tree', a local version of a Christmas tree. This may be constructed of pine branches, as there were a few planted in the area many years ago, but it is just as likely to be any other kind of branches poked into and sticking out of a banana trunk. Candles are attached to these branches and lit, resulting in a few sparks, a whole lot of singeing and occasionally the whole tree erupting into flames! We were invited to many of these gatherings and attended some, both in Salu Leäng and Tabulahan, although walking the slippery mud paths carrying children after dark is not to be recommended.

Our meals were often plain fare: usually rice with greens and dried fish, or tinned sardines and noodles on rice, or tinned mackerel or corned beef in a sauce on rice. For Christmas we were hoping to do something a little fancier. The children had been given several chickens by folk we had visited. They were a bit on the lean side, but two of them were destined to be roasted that day. We had no potatoes, but there was cassava root which tasted like potato, and Christine had brought some dehydrated peas and carrots. It was two o'clock in the afternoon before the little tin box oven on the primus stove had worked its wonders long enough and roasted the said cassava and chooks, stuffed with Delwyn's home-baked bread. It was delicious. The only problem was that our cutlery consisted of highly pliable aluminium spoons and forks, and the baked cassava skin was like rock! Christine had also brought a real Christmas pudding and custard powder. So, dessert was something special too.

We had told all our friends in the neighbourhood that we would be heading back to the city a couple of days after Christmas, but we were not expecting what happened later in the afternoon on Christmas day. The women of the congregation at Langsa', the next village after Salu Leäng, arrived armed with gifts of rice, vegetables, corn and eggs for our journey out. These kind people hardly knew us. We felt so loved.

Susan decided to spend the night of 26$^{th}$ December with Papa and Mama Tahe' down in Tabulahan. This would shorten the first day's travel for her sore feet by three kilometres. Back up the hill at Salu Leäng, the rest of us, including

Mita and Daud (two of our host's grandchildren) and a friend of theirs, set out at 7:00 the next morning. I had arranged for a horse to carry our small load of 45 kilos of bags and a man to carry Fraser. Within five minutes of setting out it was clear that the horse was barely going to make it to Tabulahan, let alone Mambi. I went on ahead to try and find a replacement horse or carriers. At Tabulahan Susan had laryngitis and was bandaging toes when I arrived. I wandered around the neighbourhood asking everyone I met if they knew of anyone with a horse. It seemed none was available. The rest of the party arrived, and we had a short prayer meeting.

Just then a young man came trotting down the hill on his horse. Someone ran after him to find out where he was off to. As it turned out, he was going to Mambi, and yes, he would be able to take our stuff if he could find a second horse, as he already had a load arranged for his own. We were pleased that the rain had held off, but we knew that it would likely start by late afternoon. After a delay the young man returned with a second horse and we were glad to be able to finally get started, however belated. The cool of the forest was welcome after a sunny morning, but we sweated up the ridge, nonetheless. At three o'clock the rain began suddenly and in earnest. It was to pour down for most of the next two hours. All sweat was sluiced and forgotten from our sodden clothing, but we were not too chilled while we walked.

At four o'clock we could walk no further. A mountain stream that we had not even noticed on the way in was now a raging torrent and completely impassable. Behind us a piece of the saturated mountainside slid down, forcing the tail-enders to scramble. There were trees all around us but none offering protection and nowhere to shelter other than under some minimally effective umbrellas. At almost 4,000 feet above sea level such conditions are cold even in the tropics. We shivered and huddled, wondering if we would have to overnight there. Fifteen-month-old Isaac sat soggily but quietly in his backpack for half an hour before he started to squirm and demanded release. The narrow path was its own stream bed and not ideal for a toddler. Delwyn nursed him for a while and he was content, probably the only one of us getting warm.

There was still another hour's walk ahead, even if we could cross the stream, and it would get dark at 6 o'clock. Knowing this, Christine silently prayed that we would be able to cross at 5:00 p.m. Before then the rain eased to drizzle, and we took turns checking the depth of the stream. On the dot of five o'clock, one of our travelling companions came back to the group and announced that it had receded enough to be safe. It was still a torrent tumbling down the hill between large boulders, but no longer waist deep. Delwyn later wrote:

> *We all went back down to see, but it didn't look great to me. But with helping hands of those more experienced we did make it across. Let me tell you I was all for singing the Hallelujah Chorus on the other side.*

An hour later, just on dusk, we climbed the last slope leading into Taora. Mama Semeng had gone to Tabulahan for the Christmas break, so we went to the house of the local church minister or *pendeta*. Like almost all of the Taora folk, he was a Bambam speaker, so we conversed in Indonesian. We sat in his spacious front room chatting with him and shivering in our wet clothes while his wife and other household members were in their large kitchen making coffee and preparing the evening meal. Fraser had shivered long enough and made his way into the kitchen to sit by the fire. We asked if we might join the rest of the *pendeta*'s household in the less formal surroundings of the hearthside, and all ended up sitting on the floor of that smoky, but much cosier room. When our hosts realised how cold we were and that we had no dry clothes with us, they lent us some sarongs. It was another half an hour before the two horses and their handler arrived with our bags. (We had already been ahead of them when they too had been stuck behind a previous stream.)

The following day, though over much easier terrain, held some similarities. We began with prayer—the *pendeta* who hosted us for the night prayed for our journey as we set out. The weather was dry in the morning; rain followed late afternoon. Susan, medicated for aches and pains, led the charge at a fast pace, feeling that she would be much slower later in the day. The horses brought up the rear and were soon some distance behind us.

It was only a week since Susan, Christine and I had travelled this trail on our way in, but the intervening rain had taken its toll. There were many landslides, either spilling onto the road, or leaving deep cracks in what remained of the road with the rest of it crumbled down the hillside. One of the log bridges had washed away, but what was one extra stream crossing among so many?

It had been raining for a while when the Mambi River came into view. It was the last and widest of the rivers we would have to cross that day and getting wider and deeper with the continuing rain. On a dry day it was shallow enough not to pose a problem, though still wide and swift. Today, we would need to cross with arms linked. Before that crossing, though, there was another landslide to negotiate. It was deep and wide and muddy. Christine lost a shoe to its suction—a shoe which then took no small effort to retrieve and was too full of mud to wear.

The first two braids of the river were shallow enough to cross individually. Then at the main flow we linked arms:

Delwyn, Susan and Mita in between the man from Salu Leäng carrying Fraser at the downstream end and me carrying Isaac at the upstream end. Christine spent some time washing out her shoes on the shingle island before the main flow and we watched anxiously from the far bank as she crossed the rest of the rising river with three others of our party. The water level was now past their waists, and they were some distance downstream by the time they safely reached the bank on our side. We headed into town to dry out at Mama Rudi's house.

An hour later I wandered back to the river's edge to see if I could spot the horses that had not yet arrived. All the braids of the river had coalesced. The island where Christine had put her shoes on had disappeared. It was clear that neither the horses, nor our dry clothing or food, would be crossing that day. We had nothing to share with our host and we would have to borrow sarongs again.

The following morning was sunny and warm, so we were able to dry our wet clothing and allow the road up ahead to dry off as well. At midday we loaded up the car with the seven adults, two children, two chickens and all the luggage. I don't remember much of that particular drive. Other times along the road between Mala'bo' and Mambi were more memorable, but Susan and Delwyn both wrote accounts.

Susan:

*It was encouraging to see that other cars had been able to get through from Mala'bo', although they estimated that it would take us five hours to negotiate the landslides and other obstacles on the road. In actual fact it only took two and a half hours. It was good to be able to follow the tracks of cars which had come in before, but even so there were times when I was hanging on to the door and praying that we wouldn't slide a foot to the left and over the edge. At* one stage I managed to find my voice and croak a warning: "No! You have half a wheel off the bridge!"

Delwyn:

*I sat in the back and every time the road up ahead looked bad, I looked behind us to see what we had covered and that made it easier to cope with. We only got stuck once. The culprit was a big rock that the underneath of the car got caught on. With the aid of a spade and jack, Robin and Daud got us free. That took about fifteen minutes. We got past the rotten little bridge which thankfully had been fortified, but we all piled out of the car just the same and left Robin to drive across, and a few kilometres later we arrived at Mala'bo'. The road was sealed from here and five minutes later the rain came down. All this was much cause for great rejoicing for answered prayers.*

# 6

# A Song in the Night

"O Mama Fraser, Papa Fraser, I just buried my child!" These were the first words we heard from Indo Datu on next reaching Salu Leäng. We were shocked. As far as we knew Pa' Pandita and his wife had two children: Papa Abri, with whom we had stayed in Polewali just three days beforehand, and Mama Ondong who lived with them here.

"Surely not Mama Ondong?" we asked hesitantly.

"No, not Mama Ondong. Our adopted daughter, Mina," Indo Datu explained through her tears. We were not aware of any adopted daughter, or at that point how common adoption was.

"Was she ill?" we asked.

"No, not ill. She gave birth to a baby twelve days ago. But the placenta did not deliver. She lived for five days after the birth. Then she died. So now we will look after her baby, just as we looked after his mother."

He was a tiny little thing. They asked us to give him a name. We hoped he might grow up to be a man of God, so we suggested 'Elia', the Indonesian name for 'Elijah'.

We observed that they were feeding him the water in which the rice was being boiled, with a little sugar added. Twice a day Mama E'bi came up from her house to wet-nurse him, as she was currently breastfeeding her three-month-old daughter,

Da'ling. Apparently, someone had been sent to the coast to buy formula milk, but it had not yet arrived.

"If it would be of any help," Delwyn offered, "I could also breastfeed the baby. I know Isaac is older and my milk is not the same as it was when he was tiny, but I am willing. Call me, even in the middle of the night if you like, since I am just downstairs."

The offer was gratefully received and Delwyn supplemented the newborn's milk supply, especially when Mama E'bi could not come, and in the night hours. The formula milk arrived after a couple of days but was only enough for a week or two, and only when it had run out completely did someone go to the coast to buy more. And the wet-nursing would begin again.

Delwyn's parents were music teachers and she had been raised in a household where music was heard from morning till night—whether her own practice and that of her siblings, or the music lessons her parents were giving to pupils. She followed a similar course, studying music at university in addition to exams for piano and other instruments. Before coming to Indonesia, she already had a keen interest in ethnomusicology: the study of music within culture. As yet she had not had opportunity to further that interest academically, but she was hoping traditional music might have been significant in the culture to which we were heading.

Now, after eight months studying the language and culture of the Tabulahan people, it seemed she was to be disappointed. Any inquiries she had made about traditional Tabulahan music were met with a "No, we don't have any traditional music anymore." The only music we commonly heard were the hymns and psalms sung in church. These were either Western hymn tunes or the psalm melodies of Dutch Reform tradition. And even young people singing with a homemade guitar on someone's front porch were singing Western tunes.

Then one evening, not long after we had arrived, we were putting our boys to bed under their mosquito net when we heard some singing. It was emanating from the kitchen upstairs and quite audible through the gaps in our walls and the kitchen floor. It was Indo Datu singing a lullaby to baby Elia. Delwyn and I looked at each other in amazement. "That's not 'Hymns Ancient and Modern'!" I remarked. Delwyn went upstairs quickly while I finished tucking the boys in.

"What song was that?" Delwyn asked our hostess.

"Oh that? That was just a song to get the baby to sleep."

"I've never heard it before. It is beautiful. Do you have any more songs like that? Not just songs to get babies to sleep, but other old songs?"

"Oh yes, there are many. But we don't sing them very much these days. Mostly just a few of the old people remember them."

"Well, we would love to hear them if we could. And we would love to record them, so they are never lost."

That request sparked a flurry of activity over the next two weeks. This was to be just a short trip to the village due to a sociolinguistics seminar in Ujung Pandang interrupting our stay. In the days that followed Delwyn's request, word got out that not only did we not disapprove of traditional music, but we also actually wanted to hear as much of it as possible. Some of the oldest members of the Salu Leäng and Langsa' villages arrived at our hosts' house to rehearse and to teach younger members of the community. Mama Ondong was the proud owner of a treadle sewing machine and put it to good use, making up some traditional ladies' costumes of red, white and black layered cloth, with a red blouse. Other women of the neighbourhood decorated these tops with dozens of white buttons.

One name we had heard a lot in the past couple of days

regarding traditional type song and dance was Pua' Pala. He, we were told, was the expert at *mangnganda'*, a male solo dance, and also at impromptu songs. He arrived along with some of the older women and took his turn rehearsing his dance, in between a mixture of older and younger women teaching and learning steps for several traditional women's songs and dances. When they were satisfied with the standard, they set off home with a promise to return on a certain day. Hopefully the weather would be better, and we would be able to record on videotape all of this material outside on the flat frontage of the Pandita's house, rather than in the dark room used for rehearsal.

The day arrived and with it the sun. It was ideal for recording outdoors, apart from the incessant background shrill of cicadas. There were perhaps a dozen women assembled and chatting excitedly in their red, white and black outfits. Four girls also arrived from across the valley in Tabulahan, dressed in similar fancy garb and carrying a couple of large gongs. Pa' Pandita came down the stairs in sarong and turban carrying a hide-covered drum. And Pua' Pala arrived also in his turban but carrying an elaborate conical headdress with flattened buffalo horns attached, and a decorated whip-like stick with bells.

The ladies demonstrated half a dozen dances accompanied by Pa' Pandita drumming a different rhythm for each. They also sang a couple of unaccompanied songs, one of which they sang standing around a suspended model boat. It commemorated their female ancestor who came by boat to meet their male ancestor who came across the mountains. Then the girls from Tabulahan danced on top of the two gongs. The highlight was Pua' Pala who danced as he sang two very different songs: first a formulaic song with buffalo headdress and whip; the second, while dressed in a turban with cloths suspended from his wrists, an impromptu song telling of how Papa and

Mama Fraser had come over the sea and over the mountains to enter the local language.

And it was not only that one day of recording. Across in the hamlet of Kombeng we visited Ambe Ale'. He was a respected old man and he remembered how to make a *tandilong*: a two-stringed instrument with a gourd sounding box. He even made one to show us, using a coconut shell in place of a gourd, and he played it as he sang us a song, the lyrics of which were about the *tandilong*.

What a rich resource we gained during those two weeks in the village! With delays and the impending sociolinguistic seminar in the city, we had even wondered if it was worth bothering to spend four days' travel in and four days' travel out again. But it turned out to be one of our most productive trips, not only in terms of all the traditional music we had discovered, but also in building relationships with the extended family through Delwyn feeding Elia, in gathering language data and in finding a few promising people to attend a translation seminar to be held in Ujung Pandang the following month. It was a reminder to seize the day and make the most of an opportunity, and to not despise small beginnings.

It was also a trip with clearly answered prayers. On the way in, the horse handlers had not secured all of the baggage properly on the saddle hooks. At one point a case fell off, bounced on a rock and into the corner of a rice field. Water had not penetrated the wrapping, but we were apprehensive as to what damage the rock may have caused the contents, namely the radio. After setting up the antenna and connecting the car battery, we switched on the radio in time for a sked. All we got was the sound of unrecognisable words. I don't mean words in a foreign language, I mean by the intonation patterns it was clearly English, but we couldn't make out a single syllable. We turned it off, prayed over it and removed the cover to see if there was anything clearly amiss inside that we might be able to fix. There wasn't anything visibly wrong. After replacing the cover, I switched it back on and, lo and behold, there was recognisable English from recognisable colleagues. It felt like a spiritual attack had just been thwarted. Cause for rejoicing and a realisation that even though this was to be a very short time, we were meant to be here.

There were so many good things we experienced that trip. But above all, Delwyn was delighted that there was still some traditional music surviving that she might use as a basis for studying their musical system. Through this she hoped to be able to encourage the development of indigenous praise songs and hymns, so that people would be able to express their worship of God in their own way, instead of only with imported styles of music.

Years later Delwyn had opportunity to attend an ethnomusicology course in Dallas where she learned to analyse musical systems. She used this acquired knowledge to better understand traditional Tabulahan music and to experiment in writing some Tabulahan songs, mostly using Tabulahan Scripture passages. This was not an end in itself. Rather she hoped these songs would become a catalyst to spark a movement of local songwriters writing their own songs and especially songs of worship.

# 7
# Bridges Built, Damaged, Repaired

The villages of Salu Leäng and Langsa' are separated from the rest of the Tabulahan-speaking area by the swift-flowing Ma'bu River. Once every few years a rainstorm is heavy enough to raise the water five metres or more, and the connecting bridge is washed away. While we had been preparing to come to the area for this trip, such a storm did its damage. Upstream several rice barns were destroyed. The same rains at Kumaka, where we had had so much trouble previously, caused a tractor to overturn, killing three people. And in Tabulahan the Ma'bu bridge released its hold on the banks and yielded to the deluge. Men of the area were quick to set about cutting the six-inch diameter bamboo necessary to rebuild the main structure, lashing it with the coarse hand-twisted rope made from sugar palm fibre.

By the time we reached the area, the newly constructed bridge was already open to foot traffic and, soon afterwards, to hoof traffic, providing again a vital link between communities. Grateful for its reconstruction, we were in the process of building our own bridges—bridges from our ignorance to an understanding of the language, bridges of communication with its speakers and bridges of relationship with government, church and community.

Officially the language is Aralle-Tabulahan, named for the two main dialect areas. We were working in the Christian area, which historically was also the ancestral home of several groups in the wider area reaching down as far as Mandar to the south and Mamuju to the west. Consequently, it was considered the prestige dialect of the language. Folk in Aralle told us that people in Tabulahan spoke the truest form of their language and by living there we had chosen the best place to learn it. Now that we were travelling in from the south, we always passed through Aralle. As we walked through its villages, we often sang of our desire to see the name of the Lord glorified in this other part of the language group.*

Although we had government permission to be living and working in Tabulahan, we were keen also to find out more about the dialectal differences in Aralle. A good opportunity arose, giving us a legitimate reason to spend time in this area. There was to be a sociolinguistic seminar for students at Hasanuddin University where I had been lecturing during our first year in Sulawesi. A few days of classroom preparation were to be followed by a week of field work, each student going to a different geographical area to study language and society in that context. I planned to leave Delwyn and the boys in Aralle on my way to Ujung Pandang. From there I would take three students and drop each one off in an area where colleagues were working and able to supervise and guide them: one in Mamasa, one in Bambam, and the third would accompany me to Aralle, as it was too far in the time frame for him to go all the way to Tabulahan.

On our way into Tabulahan two weeks earlier we had called in at the main village of Tapako and met the head of the Aralle area, which comprised at least a dozen villages. We explained to him our hope to stay there a few days and bring a student from the university. He was very accommodating and invited us to stay at his house when we came.

---

* See song: 'Come Upon These People'

It was the middle of the day, dry and hot when we arrived in Aralle, having walked 15 kilometres from Taora that morning and 21 kilometres from Salu Leäng the day before. Isaac was relieved to get out of the backpack and move around unencumbered. After lunch and seeing the family settled, I walked the remaining 11 kilometres, got in the car and overnighted with the Campbells in their village home on my way to Ujung Pandang. Delwyn, in Aralle, picks up the narrative...

*We found out that the whole village was all geared up for a wedding and I was invited if I wasn't too tired. I was grateful for something to take my mind off Robin leaving, so accepted the invitation.*

*We sat on the floor in front of the bridal couple and I was asked to have my photo taken with them early on in the proceedings. There was a band of young people singing songs, and family or friends were invited up to sing a verse there and then. In the middle of all this I heard my name, and it was announced that I was going to sing! (Nobody told me beforehand.) I explained that it would be impossible because the children were clinging to me and, anyway, I did much better with Robin. That was fine – it was worth a try, I guess they thought. Soon afterwards Isaac got up and started to dance with all the music. The crowd screamed with delight and Isaac got such a fright he headed straight for my lap. He gained confidence and tried again with the same result. Fraser was pretty tired but enjoyed seeing the wedding. The giving away of the bride was accompanied with a threat of destruction of property to the groom's family if the marriage was broken. Our host gave a rousing speech about family planning, which is a feature of weddings, it seems, as the government representative expounds the government line on keeping families to* two children. He himself has six children, a small family compared to some.

The next day was to be the start of a three-day Koran reading competition. Crowds arrived from nearby villages, and we seemed like part of the entertainment. It was all going to start on Sunday evening, so I got the boys down for afternoon sleeps so we could attend. The market area had been set up for the event and there was smoke and people everywhere. We were ushered up to the front to sit with important people like the head imam for Mambi district, heads of villages and those judging the competition. I didn't know how long the boys would last in the stifling atmosphere. Even though it was held outside, it was very hot. It took a while to get going—it was about 8:00 p.m. when it did. A young man wearing a sarong, national hat and white gloves walked upstairs to a platform that had been made for the occasion. There was a cushion on the floor, and he placed the Koran he was carrying on it, opened at a prepared place, and sat cross-legged in front of it. After a short time, he began to read it in the style of what we hear from the mosques' loudspeakers. At a prearranged signal he stopped. Soon afterwards a young woman wearing a sarong and a white veil covering all but her face also went up and did much the same. Fraser was getting restless once he was aware of all that it entailed and said he was tired and wanted to go home. Isaac was also hot and getting bothered, so we excused ourselves after the young woman finished. Everyone was understanding about the children.

Fraser had a few questions about it all and so I told him the story of Philip and the Ethiopian eunuch and how he didn't understand what he was reading, and I expounded a little on that. When I finished it seemed to be a lot clearer to him and then I prayed. As soon as I finished praying,

*Fraser spontaneously prayed for the people there, that they would come to know Him. He so rarely prays without being asked. I was quite surprised and blessed that something must have rung clear for him.*

*For the next two days I had plenty of opportunity to impress the people of Aralle with my knowledge of their language and they often complimented me on my ability. On the last night of the festivities there was to be a dance/singing competition. I was interested in seeing it but was determined to only go if the kids were up to it. Fraser was keen so I had got them down for sleeps in the afternoon. Each group had about ten girls and one main singer. Within each group they dressed the same and all wore veils, but each group varied in the colours of their skirts. It was a set song with small foot movements, and the girls accompanied themselves with tambourines. However, we only saw a little of it before Isaac and Fraser had had enough of all the attention and smoke, so we were only there for about twenty minutes.*

*When we got home, I tried to nurse Isaac, but nothing I could do would settle him. I laid him down and he just cried, so I finally (why the last resort I don't know) prayed against the attack of Satan and bound his control over Isaac. He stopped crying instantly and went to sleep. I felt really encouraged and strengthened seeing the Lord's answer so immediate and definite. I was exhausted, though, and fell asleep soon after.*

*Before coming to the village this time someone had handed us a paper written by an SIL member on the subject of spiritual warfare. It is the best thing I have ever read about it and a lot of things fell into place for us. Robin had just finished reading it in Salu Leäng and we had a neat time of prayer there covering the areas we are living and working in.*

*I took the boys to watch a volleyball game one day. During this a very forward young man came up to me to tell me that he would like to marry a European and said he felt we were 'suitable'. I just moved away, but I suddenly realised how different this society was. I could not imagine young men of Tabulahan ever making such a proposition.*

*The next day was helped along by the arrival by car from Mambi of the doctor there and his team of officials and nurses. They administered family planning methods to the women of the area. Government officials from Mambi had organised a team to move boulders in the river at a point where a car might cross it and generally improve the state of the road sufficiently to allow a 4WD to get through. (We never tried to take our car across, knowing that a decent rainfall would prevent our departure for who knew how long.) I asked the doctor why he never came to Tabulahan, as that is also a part of the Mambi district. He replied that he had so many patients he could only go to those that could be reached by car. I suppose that is fair enough, given that he is the only doctor in an area of 50,000 people.*

*The boys had times of enjoying and disliking all the attention they received. But both liked the animals. Isaac particularly liked the ducks and the goat next door. Fraser was impressed with the speed of a 3-week-old buffalo calf. He said, "See that baby buffalo, Mummy. He can run. He really can! But not as fast as a spaceship yet."*

*There were several things that really helped me in Aralle. For one thing, the house had a bathroom area consisting of a* bak\* *and concrete floor, so although most people went down to the river to do washing and bathing, it was easier for me to just do all that up at the house, particularly at*

---

\* *bak*: a bathroom water container for showering with a dipper.

*times when the kids were both fairly clingy with all the people who wanted to feel their hair and pinch their skin. Another thing was the food—we all enjoyed it and ate well. Nights went pretty well too. If Isaac woke it was usually only once for a quick drink. I think it was because he was eating well during the day. We also had two Sundays here. There is a little group of Bambam speakers in the Aralle area who have a church which was quite close, so we went there and ate with them after the services.*

*One thing I learnt in a new way was the power of praise. When I felt the pressure of the kids' needs and was not able to meet them (e.g., when they were so hungry and tired and I was not able to feed them nor get them to bed early enough), or just the pressure of being with strangers of a different religion in a new place, it was as if I could just cut through it all as I reached out to the Lord with a song of praise. I was very conscious that there must have been lots of prayers for us from folk back home too.*

After dropping off the other students in Mamasa and Bambam, I arrived back in Aralle with my student, a young Bugis man from Pinrang. He was just in time for the Friday prayers at the local mosque. So, while he went to pray, I was able to catch up with Delwyn and the boys.

Over the following days I toured around with my student. While he was gathering data for his project, I was able to ask my own questions relating to dialectal differences between Tabulahan and Aralle. Delwyn had already begun to note down anything different she had heard while I had been away. These notes were a great start and, coupled with my own notes, gave me some fuel for a paper I was in process of writing on the phonology of the language. I also was able to record a text in Aralle of a story I had already recorded in Tabulahan and was looking forward to picking through dialectal differences from this.

It felt so good to be reunited with the family, and I think it was a more relaxing time for them also after I got back. I was thankful to our host for the good care he had taken of these strangers, my family, while I had been away. Above all we were all thankful to the Lord for his sustaining love for us in yet another situation.

\*\*\*\*

After leaving Aralle, we headed to Mamasa, where there was a meeting with the church leadership scheduled for each of the three language teams working in the area. Ron, our director, also travelled up from Ujung Pandang for the meeting. It was a somewhat formal meeting and there was tension in the air, with one member dominating the discussion. His opinion was that for the sake of church unity, there should only be one Scripture translation undertaken in the area. That there were significant differences between the three languages where the church had membership did not seem to matter to him—they could all use the Mamasa translation as far as he was concerned. The rest of the church leaders present followed his line. We left the meeting with heavy hearts. Neither we in Tabulahan, nor the Mattis in Mamasa, were ready to begin translation at that point, but the Campbells in Bambam were. And how, we wondered, would the three communities react to this decision from the church hierarchy?

Far from being a good decision in terms of church unity, it seemed the meeting's conclusion brought division—a wall, rather than a bridge. The reaction of church members in both Tabulahan and Bambam was quite indignant. They thought it made no sense. Why would they want to use a Mamasa translation if the goal was to understand the Word of God better? They might as well continue to use the Indonesian translation. At least they had had some schooling in that language. Some even said there was no way they would ever buy a Mamasa translation. It seemed this was yet another unsubtle attack of the enemy to prevent the Word of God being understood. We prayed for the Lord to intervene if He wanted us to continue the work we had begun.

Such lively discussions in the villages fostered a greater interest in the projects than there had been to date. There was a new determination that there should be three translations, whether approved of from the leadership in Mamasa or not. Eventually, when this news reached the synod leaders, they rethought the issue and formally invited the three teams to work towards three translations, one for each of the three languages. And bridges were repaired.

# 8

# In Sickness and Health

Our next time in the village was again productive in terms of language learning and building relationships. It was a sad time, though, with a lot of sickness and several deaths in the community. We hadn't even reached the village when we were asked to take with us the sad news of the death of a high school girl who was studying outside the area. We heard that she had taken her own life by drinking insecticide. The whole community was shocked and her mother distraught. Sadly, there was to be more tragedy.

From our earliest days in the area, we were often asked for medicines, some of which we routinely carried for our own use and were able to give out when our supply allowed. These were generally drugs like paracetamol for headache and fever, chloroquine for malaria and mebendazole for worm infestations. Some of the other medicines requested we were also able to procure in the city and bring in specifically for people who needed them.

One of the most common ailments, particularly among women, was goitre. The Tabulahan soil lacked iodine, and the salt sold in the markets was not iodised. We could buy iodised salt in the city for about the same price as the un-iodised village salt, so we made a habit of bringing in a horse-load each time. However, the cost of hiring the horse was more than the cost of the salt, so we abandoned this practice once we discovered that we could buy iodine tablets at a pharmacy in Ujung Pandang. After a few years the incidence and severity of goitre had reduced considerably.

Chest ailments were also very common, due in large measure no doubt to all members of the community spending a lot of time in smoky kitchens without windows or chimneys—that, and the fact that almost all of the men smoked cigarettes. Consequently, we were often asked for cough medicines, which we never dished out without an accompanying warning on the dangers of smoking.

Sometimes it was an injury that we were asked to help with. We did not have a great first aid kit, but it was more than anyone else there had. One day a young man came limping to us with a great machete gash between his toes that needed stitching. We had no local anaesthetic, nor any proper instruments, but if he was brave and willing, I would give it a go. He was, so I did. I cleaned the wound as best I could, poured in a pile of antibiotic powder and sewed it up with some waxed thread and a heavy sewing needle. He didn't utter a sound. I'd forgotten all about this until Fraser visited the area a few years ago and a man eagerly showed him the scar where Papa Fraser had done his needlework.

There was no clinic in the Tabulahan area at that time. If anyone got seriously sick, they would either call one of the local traditional practitioners who dealt out a mixture of herbal remedies and magic rituals, or they might send someone to bring medicine from the clinic run by a nurse and a health worker in Aralle 40 kilometres away. (This was where the doctor from Mambi held his family planning clinics two or three times a year.)

There was also a health worker who had had some medical training and was living in Sodangan, only 30 kilometres away. From time to time, he was even back home in Salu Leäng for a few weeks and able to dispense an assortment of drugs from there. It was during this, our fourth time of staying in the area, that I first encountered him.

Two weeks into our time in the village I left Delwyn and the boys in Salu Leäng while I again travelled to Mambi for a meeting with church leaders. I had previously never taken the slightly shorter but much steeper route over Pote' Leha. It was a steep trail and over a thousand feet higher than the highest point of our usual route. I thought on the way that I'd never want to take the family over that mountain. This route also missed Taora, where we usually overnighted, but I'd been told that I should ask for the *mantiri*, or health worker, in Sodangan and stay at his place.

The *mantiri* was not there when I arrived mid-afternoon at the village. Someone directed me to his house: a rough looking shack with a dirt floor and a raised sleeping area. There was a married couple inside. The man informed me that he was there for a few months while being treated for tuberculosis. His wife was also there to do all the cooking and cleaning as payment for the medicines. The *mantiri*, he told me, had gone off to get *tuak\** from his sugar palm. He'd be back before nightfall. I gave the man's wife the food I had brought to share.

Sure enough, at about 5:30 p.m. as I was sitting in the shade outside the door, along came the health worker dressed in an old army trench coat, with a fat bamboo tube held in place on his back by a thin rattan strap. It looked like he was having trouble keeping his feet quite in line, but that may have been due to the oversized laceless boots. I stood and introduced myself, shook his hand and told him I was on my way to Mambi. After a few "What did you say?"s and cupping his hand to his ear, I realised that he was quite deaf, as well

---

\* An alcoholic drink from the fermented sap of the sugar palm.

as more than a little inebriated. The consumptive house guest came to my aid and shouted what I had been saying, and the *mantiri* nodded and went inside.

I followed after a minute or two. The patient's wife was squatting by the fire in the kitchen, blowing at the embers under the blackened pot. The patient was reminding the *mantiri* that it was time for his shot. I was wondering where this might take place, or indeed where any medicines might be stored. The only cupboard was a rough plank affair, not unlike the one we had built in Salu Leäng. This now the health worker wrenched open and a dozen cockroaches skittered for cover in as many directions. He picked up the syringe lying on the shelf, stuck the needle into a bottle, drew some liquid and squirted a little into the air. Then he spun around on one foot and, while still balancing on that one foot, with a grin on his face and his trench coat flapping at his sides, bent over and stabbed the needle into the exposed buttock of the patient. The patient rubbed the point of impact, pulled up his trousers and went to join his wife in the kitchen. The *mantiri* put the syringe into the cupboard and went outside to have another drink.

After dinner, while we were clearing dishes in the kitchen, a voice was heard through the wall and a man came in from the dark. He said his wife was very sick, too sick to travel, so he had walked since dawn to come for medicine for her. This was all shouted for the benefit of the deaf health worker. He asked the man to describe his wife's condition and a vague summary of fever and pain in various places ensued. The *mantiri* went back to the cupboard and the cockroaches danced away again from the light. From several jars he began to tip pills of various colours into a transparent plastic bag. It looked not unlike a packet of liquorice all sorts. "Here," he said. "Give her these." The man turned to leave. "Are you leaving already?" the *mantiri* asked, "I thought you would be leaving in the morning."

"No, I must get back. I'll go straight away."

"Okay, go carefully then."

The man paused in the doorway. "How many is she to take at once." All eyes were focused on the jumble of pills rattling around in the plastic bag.

The health worker examined them and thought for a few seconds. "The red ones… one, twice a day. The blue ones… er… three a day. The white ones whenever she is in pain. And the black and green ones…er… four, once a day. No. One, four times a day. Okay?"

"Yeah, I think so," the man said and bowed out into the night.

Meanwhile back in Salu Leäng, Delwyn had attended a funeral in the hamlet of Panampo. We did not know the deceased, but apparently, he had been left a widower twice and was the father of six children. His eldest daughter was now breastfeeding her youngest sister as well as her own son. The only man of the family was her younger brother who was lying on a mat, sick with malaria. After the funeral Delwyn called in on them and was glad to find she had chloroquine in her bag with her, which she was able to leave with the sick young man.

Next day she wrote:

*I was struck last night as I meditated on John 1:1-14 just how special each person is to God. I was reminded afresh of how intricately we are made. I long for a compassionate heart towards the people here so that I can respond to them the way Jesus would.*

Sometimes it is our own pain that best helps us empathise with others' suffering. A couple of days after I got back from Mambi, while we were visiting folk in one of the Salu Leäng hamlets, Delwyn hurried back up the hill from the hamlet of Bulung, wanting to change into old clothes to help the ladies planting rice down there. Still in a rush back at the house, she thought she had better do the washing before heading out again. While squatting on the washing rock she developed abdominal pain that she described as on a level with childbirth and almost passed out. She took some paracetamol and lay down, calling out to the folk upstairs to have someone go and fetch me from Bulung. Meanwhile, five-year-old Fraser prayed for her, thanking Jesus that she would get better. Indeed, she did. But as she lay in pain she thought about our isolation and later wrote:

> *It made me realise just how far we are from help if anything happened. It also makes me realise that we have to trust the Lord for our health. Later Robin and I talked about what we would do if one of us felt so ill we needed to leave in a hurry.*

From time to time each of us did get sick—most commonly stomach complaints from something we had eaten or drunk. We all suffered intermittently from worms, lice, bedbugs and other parasites. Or sometimes one of us had a fever that we had no way of identifying. I think I might have had malaria at one point, but I am not sure. Next to the Bible, the book *Where There is no Doctor* was our most leafed through source when looking for guidance. These days, where there *is* a doctor, people still try to self-diagnose online, and we had no other option. The problem is that symptoms may point to more than one cause, and this can sometimes lead to a wrong diagnosis.

One time I was concerned that a swollen lymph node in the groin might have been a hernia, due to other accompanying symptoms. *Where There is no Doctor* left me with both options.

Someone upstairs heard about this and sent for a respected church elder over in Kombeng who was considered the local expert on hernias. He arrived, examined me and decided that it was not a hernia, but a swollen lymph node, most likely due to the small wound on my foot. He then proceeded to offer the local cure: a machete heated by the fire until sufficiently hot and then pressed, not on the wound, but on the lymph node! I thanked him for the diagnosis but declined the treatment and started on a course of antibiotics. He still felt he needed to do something helpful before he left so offered me a back massage. He rubbed my back with half an onion and, before I realised what he was doing, mumbled incantations. We prayed against any negative spiritual effects afterwards.

But we were generally healthy and did have a greater resistance to a lot of the local maladies than the general populace. We ate a good, varied diet in town and supplemented the village diet with a few items brought in. Most in the community around us did not have as varied a diet. The average person's meal in Tabulahan consisted of a lot of rice (apart from a month or so before harvest when root crops and corn meal became substitute staples) and usually some leafy greens boiled with salt. Extra protein could be derived from salty dried fish, bony rice field fish, or an egg. But most people would not eat any of these on a daily basis—perhaps only two or three times a week. And meat was only served for special occasions, like a chicken cooked for a visitor from afar; or a pig, cow or buffalo butchered for a wedding or a funeral.

Across the area it was customary to give a chicken to a child on their first visit to a household, or an egg if no chicken was available. Langsa' was the next village after Salu Leäng. It was one of the poorest in the area, but the people were as kind and hospitable as any from the slightly less poor villages. We always enjoyed our visits there. Perhaps the poorest household among them was that of Indo Uli. Her house was a tiny shack of about 2.4 by 2.4 metres (about 62 square feet) in which she lived with her mother and her four children. Her husband had already died. On our first visit there, Indo Uli had given us two young chickens, one for each of the boys. They were their only chickens, and we were reluctant to take them but knew it would be offensive to refuse.

We went to visit Indo Uli during this trip and discovered that her eight-year-old daughter was sick. Ati was a lovely young girl who had often come over to our place for a visit. She was able to sit up but was clearly not well, very thin and her face looking puffy and pale. It seemed to us that she was lacking in protein. Probably the whole family was. We visited again and took mung beans and eggs from the chickens, asking her mother to make sure Ati ate plenty and to send another child over each week to get more. But we don't think any of it was getting to her. Her grandmother said one time, "No point wasting it on her, she is going to die."

And she did. It broke our heart that this lovely young girl had such a short life. I was again out of the area on my way to Ujung Pandang to pick up my brother and sister-in-law. Delwyn wrote:

> *Jul 31$^{st}$, I knew as soon as I heard the bell ring out of the ordinary that someone had died. It was coming from Langsa' and I soon learned that it was our little friend Ati… I've been churning it all over in my mind. Did what we gave the family for her get to her? Or did she have something else other than malnutrition? It was less than a week ago that I gave her more eggs and mung beans. I wish I had given milk too. Or was it something spiritual? Did I pray amiss when we visited? Maybe we didn't pray enough. I really wish Robin was here to share these thoughts.*

*Aug 1ˢᵗ, On arrival at Ati's house I was overcome with it all and had a good weep as I sat in their little house. This was the first person that we have known well that has died here. And it seemed so unnecessary.*

As the two pallbearers took the small, rough plank coffin from the house, a third man killed a young chicken by bashing it on the coffin lid. He then threw it away outside. This, Delwyn was told, was to prevent the sickness from remaining in the house.

A not uncommon cause of death was complications around childbirth. Childbirth was something to be feared by women. Although there would usually be an older female relative in attendance at a birth, any complications could not be easily dealt with, and any clinic was too far away to reach. We know of several cases where women died from a retained placenta. Perhaps the saddest thing we ever saw in the village was the form of a young, heavily pregnant woman under a sheet. She had struggled in labour for six days before finally dying along with her child. Of course, most births had no such complications. Some went well even with no outside attendants. One of our near neighbours in Salu Leäng, a mother of several children, gave birth to twins in the middle of the night, only waking her husband to light the fire after the first was safely born, and then having no difficulty with the second, born feet first!

But most health issues had nothing to do with reproduction. One of the first three Tabulahan men we had met on the road while we were stuck in the forest during our first trip in was Yona. One day we heard that this young man was sick, so sick that the family was gathering. We made it a priority to go and visit him that day as we were to be leaving in a day or so. We found him with a fever, very weak and lying on a mat.

Delwyn told him that she would make him a pumpkin cake, but he would have to get better and come up to our house for it. We chatted with his family members for a while, prayed for him and sang a song.

Pua' Lenong's wife was also sick at about that time and the family had gathered as they thought the end was near. She was in her sixties and had been sick for a while and then had stopped eating altogether. Again, we called in, prayed and sang a song of praise. Back at home Delwyn had an inspiration. She emptied a can of sweetened condensed milk into a screw-top jar so as to be resealable and took it down to the family, suggesting that the invalid might like to try a spoonful in a glass of hot water. We left the village soon after, not knowing if we would see either Yona or Pua' Lenong's wife again.

On our next trip into the village Yona was back to good health and able to get his pumpkin cake. And Pua' Lenong dropped by our place one day. "Oh, Mama Fraser," he said. "That medicine that you gave my wife was good stuff. She liked it, she started eating again and she grew strong." (Just a few weeks ago as I write this, and more than twenty years after that incident, we met her again at a memorial service for her husband, Pua' Lenong, who had recently died. It was good to see Yona fit and healthy at the same time.)

# 9

# A Family Visit

During those first two years of living in Indonesia we were blessed by the visits of our missions pastor and his wife, two of Delwyn's three sisters, her mother, and my parents. Each of these visits happened during times of living in the city of Palu (although Delwyn's mother also helped with childcare at a conference in Tabo-Tabo). No one other than a select few colleagues had visited us while we were living in the villages of Tabulahan.

That changed when my brother, Fraser, and his wife, Lesa, added an Indonesian stopover to their long-planned trip to Europe. So, as Delwyn and the boys were attending Ati's funeral, I was en route to Ujung Pandang after the two-day walk to Mambi where we had left the car. Several Tabulahan folk asked if I could give them a lift down to Polewali on my way. I had room for the six passengers, so they piled in. Some had never been in a car before, and all suffered from travel sickness. In the glove box were a few plastic bags which came in handy soon after we began moving. Once used, each of the vomiting passengers immediately threw the bag out of the window. In no time we had run out of bags and the vomiting was directed either straight out of the window or into a sarong held on the lap. Of course, the sarong could not be thrown away and the smell lingered all the way down to Polewali.

It was late in the day when Fraser and Lesa's flight from

Denpasar, Bali landed at the airport in Ujung Pandang, so we drove into town and overnighted at the Campbell's house. The Campbells were in the village at the time, but Dorkas, their domestic helper, made sure we were well looked after. Overnighting in Ujung Pandang also gave me the opportunity to have a radio sked with Delwyn, who was worried about whether I had made it past the Mambi road. In fact, the road out had been wet and muddy, but not terrible, apart from a few tricky bits.

On the drive north out of town Fraser and Lesa were absorbing all the sights of a culture so different from anything they had experienced before. So many of these things had been novel and wonderful for us two years beforehand, but now had been relegated to being just part of the background scenery.

Fraser spotted a roadside seller with a stack of green coconuts. "What are those green things?"

"Coconuts."

"Really? I thought coconuts were small, brown and hairy."

"Well, these ones are young coconuts, newly picked, still in their husks."

"Oh, right."

A few kilometres further along the road he spotted another seller. "What are those orange things?"

"Coconuts."

"Wow! I thought coconuts were green."

"Well, some are, but these are orange. They might be a hybrid variety." And so it went on with questions and comments on the pomelos, the salaks and other fruit being sold; on the cross-over gable ends of the Bugis houses; on the limestone karsts of Maros district; on buffalos bathing in the sea at a creek mouth. It was wonderful to be a tour guide for people clearly interested, and especially to have someone as reactive as my brother Fraser being wowed by everything he saw.

Again, in Polewali we swapped the road wheels for wheels with mud tyres, and my guests were able to meet Papa Abri and his family there. At a curve in the road north of Polewali there is an interesting traditional-style Mamasan house, with its upcurved roof ends and decorated front panels. This again extracted a "Wow!" from my brother, as it had for us when we first drove this road.

It was raining by the time we reached Mala'bo', and the Land Cruiser started to earn its 4WD keep. The road had worsened over the past two days and there were a few places where driving needed serious concentration. By halfway to Mambi the rain was really hammering down, and visibility was reduced to not far beyond the leading edge of the car's hood. Fraser had brought a video camera. This would have been a great opportunity to get out and film the road on one of its worse days. But of course, when the weather is that bad you don't want to drown your camera. Filming would have to wait for the balmy weather of the trip out when the mud had mostly dried up.

I had organised a horse to carry Fraser and Lesa's bags. It was a *balibi*, a beautiful chestnut colour—probably the sleekest, healthiest horse we ever used. Dalle', the horse's owner, was an outgoing young man, very keen to engage the newcomers in conversation. That meant a lot of translating on my part for the two-day walk along the trail, as Dalle' had no English and Fraser and Lesa had no Tabulahan nor Indonesian. Lesa mentioned that she had been learning some NZ sign language for signing songs for the deaf members of their congregation. When Dalle' heard this, he intimated that he also knew some local sign language and wondered if it was the same in New Zealand as it was in the local context. We tried a few words. Some were remarkably alike—if not conveying the same meaning, at least pointing to a cultural equivalent. For example, the NZ sign for a bicycle proved to be the Tabulahan sign for a horse. Every few minutes Dalle' would think of something else he wanted to say, ask me how to say it in English and in sign language. I would ask Lesa for an approximate equivalence, and Dalle' would use the NZ sign symbols accompanied by a barbarised pronunciation of English. In the same way, Fraser was trying Tabulahan expressions, sometimes with the aid of signs. One sentence that lives long in the memory was practised by Fraser and Dalle' at the end of the first day. The sentence: *Marondong tehte' pitu la mao tau ungngola lalang* (Tomorrow at seven o'clock we will go along the road) became, in Fraser's mouth: *MaRONdong Tek-Tek BEE-Too maLAU Tau ung-GOla LANGalang*. And in the mouth of Dalle': TuMOra SEMbeklok wi wi GUA alonga WUA.

At Taora, after a day's walk, we were hosted by Mama Semeng as usual. She had been pleased when I passed through five days earlier to have some 'meat' to offer at the evening meal. It resembled something between sugar cubes and blobs of blancmange. It was, in fact, cubes of unnaturally white pig fat and was getting past its due-by date when I partook of that meal. Now, five days later, knowing I would be returning with my brother and sister-in-law, she had kept some in reserve. It was placed in the centre of the table between the colander of rice, the bowl of spinach and the plate of chillies.

"What's that smell?" Fraser asked.

"That's the meat."

"Meat? What meat? I don't see any meat."

"That white stuff."

"That's meat?! Well, I'm not having any!"

I boldly put one piece of pig fat on my rice and spinach, tried several times to swallow it, gagging at each attempt. In the end I pulled out my handkerchief, coughed into it and returned the package to my pocket. The rest of the meal went down effortlessly, though the chillies were among the hottest I have ever eaten. Poor Fraser spent most of the meal trying to quench the furnace his mouth had become. Wisely, Lesa avoided all the controversial elements of the meal. Mama Semeng came in from the kitchen and asked why we weren't eating the meat. Before we'd had time to reply, she cheerily answered her own question. "It must be because it stinks." And with that she whisked it off to the kitchen where the other members of the household polished it off as part of their meal. After dinner we went down to the stream for an icy shower under a bamboo pipe. And I was able to dispense with my handkerchief's contents.

Once in the village, Fraser and Lesa settled into their upstairs room, as Christine and Susan had done, and spent most of their time downstairs with us in our tiny apartment. I soon put Fraser's electrical skills to work, rigging up a solar panel on the roof and a couple of 12v solar-powered fluorescent tubes in the kitchen/living area. These were a source of amazement to many of our visitors who had never come across electric lights before.

Fraser and Lesa continued to be good sports: trying new foods, despite the Taora experience; wearing sarongs like everyone else; socialising in smoky kitchens, markets and after formal church services. In short: sampling all that village life offered. On a visit to Langsa' there was to be a small display of traditional dancing and song. Fraser, who regularly plays drums at his church, squatted down to try his hand at Tabulahan-style drumming. He got some great rhythms going, although striking horizontally both skins of a single drum standing on its edge felt very different to striking downwards on a snare, cymbals and toms arranged above and around a kick drum.

Over the years Fraser and Lesa have had a succession of animals: frogs, rabbits, budgies, dogs, cats (domestic and feral!), chickens, turkeys, cows, pigs and sheep. At that time of visiting us in Tabulahan they hadn't yet experienced all of those, but took interest in all the local livestock, especially those not normally seen back home, such as water buffalo, and even those commonly seen back home, but treated differently or behaving differently from the expected. They saw skinny cats sitting in the ashes of fireplaces with tails docked (as is often done to sheep and certain dog breeds in NZ), and dogs running in and out of houses and churches and toilet areas eating anything they could find. It was rare for anyone to name their dog—they were after all livestock, destined one day to become a meal—but Fraser decided the household dog should be called 'Hoover' as he was such an efficient vacuum cleaner.

The other Fraser, our son, was crazy about flying from a very early age. And it was about this time that he went through a phase of pretending to fly by jumping off chairs, banks and rocks with great gusto. One day he fell out of a tree and landed awkwardly because he forgot 'to fly'. Fortunately, he was back climbing again in no time. Little brother copied his older brother in many things and decided flying was a good game. However, Isaac's flying consisted of dropping down from standing to an all-fours crouch. Imitation is also a wonderful language learning tool, and the little mimic was quickly picking up Tabulahan alongside Indonesian and English.

As our two guests were scheduled to fly from Jakarta to Europe, we thought it would be a good opportunity for us to see Java, the heart of the country we had been living in for two years but never visited. Again, we overnighted in Taora on the way out. In addition to the six of us and a couple of guys with horses carrying our stuff, there was a party of primary school children and accompanying teachers on their way back from singing competitions in Mambi. All converged on Mama Semeng's place that afternoon. With the four middle-schoolers boarding there and the lady of the house herself, that made 55 of us looking for a meal and a place to stay. Golden-hearted Mama Semeng didn't flinch but cooked up a storm with the help of her boarders and bedded almost all of us down for the night. It was wall to wall bodies all over the floor. Our hostess, bless her, wouldn't listen to the idea of Fraser and me sleeping on the floor, insisting that Fraser and Lesa have one of the two double beds and our family have the other.

We reached Ujung Pandang and made our flight to Jakarta in time for their international connection. Our plan was to travel overland through Java to Surabaya before flying back to Sulawesi. However, Delwyn had a broken tooth and had been experiencing toothache for some time. Here was an opportunity to get it treated and the crown it needed in Jakarta, rather than some temporary fix in Palu. So, we spent the next ten days in the capital in between dental appointments. We didn't get to see Java, but there was plenty to see within and around the city. With Delwyn newly crowned, we flew directly back to Ujung Pandang where we had left the car.

\*\*\*\*

Up to this point we had always flown between Palu in Central Sulawesi and Ujung Pandang in South Sulawesi en route to and from the village. Initially when we started work in Tabulahan there had been no connecting road either through the centre of the island or up the coast. Now that we knew the link was complete, we decided to drive up to Palu rather than flying.

A year before, I had flown down from Palu to Ujung

Pandang to accompany Mike Edwards in his Land Rover through the then newly opened Central Sulawesi section of the Trans-Sulawesi Highway. Mike and Lyn were moving up to Palu to take on the position of administrator for the Central Sulawesi teams, but Lyn didn't fancy the two-to-three-day drive with their two young ones. I was keen to see what this new 'highway' was like beyond the junction where we regularly continued on to Polewali and then Mambi. Turning east at Pare-pare, Mike and I crossed the South Sulawesi peninsula to the Bay of Bone, driving through Palopo to Wotu and turning north to Mangkutana. The road was great: narrow but sealed and no worse than the coastal highway we usually drove that reached to just beyond Mamuju.

After overnighting in a cheap roadside inn, we hit the road for the second day and began a series of newly paved switchbacks. At the top of the rise the paving petered out and the road continued unsealed and narrowed to one lane. Virgin jungle pressed in, at times brushing the Land Rover's sides. We continued for 50 kilometres or so, bouncing over rocks and tree roots until the forest thinned, and a flat landscape of scrub and tall grasses emerged. The track appeared to continue straight into this, but after only a hundred metres it was clear that this was a swamp and not the road at all. We backtracked and skirted the forest edge and rediscovered the road halfway around the swamp. It was still unsealed but had been graded and was in good condition though narrow.

A group of men flagged us down by the side of a fuel tanker. It had slipped off the soft road shoulder and was lying on its side. The men had managed to pump all of the diesel into drums to lighten its weight and now they hoped that Mike's Land Rover might be able to tow it upright. The road was far too narrow for a direct pull with a towrope, but someone suggested we loop the rope around a tree opposite the truck and reverse up the road. We both knew this would be futile but complied with the request anyway. With all four wheels spinning and rope straining, everyone concurred that they would have to await a crane, and we continued on our way. The Central Sulawesi road proved to be of similar quality to that of South Sulawesi: a few rough patches that needed reworking, but mostly sealed and just wide enough for vehicles to pass each other. We reached Palu late in the evening: 1,000 kilometres in 32 hours of actual driving—not too bad!

Now, a year later, armed with that previous experience and the questionable intelligence that the road in the border area had been worked on, we set out as a family. Friends in Ujung Pandang warned us, "You're what? You're kidding! You'll be sorry!"

We weren't. It was a pleasant two-and-a-half-day drive and a great family time, although Delwyn's teeth were still causing her a bit of grief. The road had indeed been worked on. The boys took the car journey in their stride (that said, we had to keep Isaac dosed with 'Antimo', knowing how bendy the road was), and it took nine hours less driving time than the trip with Mike had. I was excited. This meant we would be able to buy village supplies in Palu and avoid the hassles of airports and big city traffic en route to Tabulahan. This was to become our route for the foreseeable future.

Back in Palu we had a few weeks before our next time in the village. This was just as well, as Delwyn was still very tired from the stress of extra travel and dental work. It soon came out that she had developed shingles. For the next few weeks, she was very low, constantly tired and irritable. After recovering she wrote:

> *It was a dry, depressing, homesick time in Palu. Shingles really was awful. I've never been so miserable and full of*

> such self-hate and such little self-worth. I felt like going home but was fearful of that somehow too. I must have been pretty homesick though as I had so many dreams about New Zealand or people there.

Ron and Patti McCullough, OMF friends, were staying with us at the time. They had had the house to themselves while we had been in the village, but graciously dealt with the McKenzie invasion and it was a real blessing to have their support before they headed back to the UK. Besides praying for Delwyn's recovery, we were continuing to pray for the safe arrival of Fraser's first six-month shipment of correspondence school materials. This finally arrived from New Zealand, almost six months after being sent, but in time for us to begin the next chapter of village living with the new home-schooling experience.

# 10

# Questions

After a tiring six-day journey we arrived back in Salu Leäng to find Indo Datu, our hostess, sick with what we think must have been a heart condition. She was experiencing some chest pain, shortness of breath and her feet were swelling. An 'aunt' was visiting from a village a day's walk away. I had passed through that village once on my way to Mambi and knew it to be peopled by Bambam speakers who strongly held to their animistic beliefs and practices. We later found out that this 'aunt' was considered to be the most powerful shaman in the wider area. And here she was performing her rituals on the minister's wife. After giving her patient some concoction to sip, she poured the remainder on Indo Datu's head, back and chest to a muted mumbling. There was an apologetic look in Indo Datu's eyes when she saw us sitting there, as if she knew we would not approve. We understood the desperation she and her family must have felt to have called this woman when there was no hospital nor clinic, no doctor nor pharmacist. But there was prayer available. And indeed, people were praying. Her husband prayed for her, we prayed for her, and others were probably praying too. But we could not avoid the niggling thought that should she recover, which power would get the glory when opposing powers were being invoked?

The main focus of this time in the village was orthography testing. The language had not been written previously and so a writing system needed to be developed—one that would fit the phonemes and the changes these phonemes made in various contexts, as well as one that would be acceptable by the community as a good way of expressing their language in written form. The national language uses a Roman script, as we do in English, so any orthography we came up with would need to be based on this.

So, besides working on a paper for a forthcoming grammar workshop, I spent the next few weeks going around the community taking passages of text written in different ways to see which most people preferred and, more importantly, which caused the least amount of stumbling among readers. In each of the villages we visited several households with testing materials. As well as this, there were impromptu visits to our own house by villagers which gave me further opportunities to test the materials. One of these visitors was a native Tabulahan man who was headmaster in a Bambam-speaking village several hours away. He was very interested in the process and the materials we had prepared, as well as the texts and conversations we had collected and transcribed. "I'm 52 years old," he said, "and I've studied Indonesian and a bit of English. Only now am I reading my own language for the first time!"

---

### Working on the orthography: a few of the basic decisions

To begin with in our early days of language learning we had written everything in phonetic script, recording each sound with a unique symbol. After a while it became clear that some of these sounds could be grouped together as each occurred only in certain sound contexts and did not distinguish meaning from a similar sound found in a different context. An example of this was [r], which only occurred between vowel sounds, and [d], which only occurred at the beginning of words or next to a consonant sound. So, both could be represented by the one symbol, in the same way that we use the letter 'p' to represent the three different [p] sounds we use in English (perhaps without realising that we do so, for example: *p*ar (aspirated), s*p*ar (unaspirated) sa*p* (unreleased)).

Whenever we came across a 'minimal pair', that is a pair of words with different meanings that only differ in one pair of similar sounds, we rejoiced that here was clear evidence that both these sounds were significant and therefore phonemes of the language. Both would need to be written. An example of this in English is 'pig' and 'fig': the similar sounds [p] and [f] show a contrast in meaning and therefore both /p/ and /f/ need to be written. In Tabulahan, though we heard both [p] and [f], they never made any difference in meaning and so only one needed to be written. We chose to use /p/. After working through all the sounds people made in Tabulahan speech and isolating what constituted the phonemes of the language, we wrote every new expression we heard using this simpler phonemic script.

But there were other decisions that had to be made. Sounds were regularly influenced by the succeeding sounds, not only by the initial sound of the following word, but often by suffixes within a word. For example: the word for 'house' is *dasang*; the suffixes for 'my', 'your', 'his' are *-ku*, *-mu*, *-na* respectively, but while *dasangku* is the correct form for 'my house', *dasangmu* and *dasangna* are not the correct forms for 'your house' or 'his house'. The succeeding sounds of the suffixes influence the final sound of the root word, so every Tabulahan speaker will say *dasammu and dasanna*. The most efficient writing system would not record these changes or surface forms but write only the underlying forms.

However, we could not make these decisions in isolation. Community involvement was key to the orthography being accepted. Regarding the sound changes at morpheme boundaries, the consensus was that the surface form should be retained within words (so *dasammu*, not *dasangmu* should be written), but not across word boundaries, where there would be so many possible sound changes as to make the writing system unwieldy and reading complicated.

We did not require the full 26 letters used by the national language (in fact the national language could function just as well with a couple less), but there was a need for two additional sounds to be represented: something to represent a glottal stop [ʔ] and something to represent a sixth vowel sound [æ]. For the first of these, 'q' was rejected, and an apostrophe was chosen.* For the second, 'æ' and 'ä' were rejected and 'ä' was chosen. Although, as mentioned above, [r] did not need to be written, almost everyone insisted that it be so.

---

* In Indonesian, [ʔ] is represented by 'k' when found in syllable-final positions. This could never work for Tabulahan with its many vowel-initial suffixes and enclitics.

Delwyn, meanwhile, was coming to grips with being a home-schooling mother with the distractions of a two-year-old and an endless succession of visitors. A typical day she recorded as follows:

*Monday 22ⁿᵈ October. Another busy day, but also enjoyable. If I had have had today several months ago, I would not have said enjoyable, but downright stressful. It's just that we are now far more aware of what is expected of us and what is best to do in a given situation. This morning I was making bread after the sked before school (radio still seems the same ☺) and the Semengs arrived and agreed to do some orthography testing with Robin. Fraser was ready to do school and Isaac was content, fortunately. So, while Robin started with Papa Semeng, I sat down with Mama Semeng. She was eager to have my pumpkin cake recipe and also wanted some of the ingredients I had to get her going on her own. Fortunately, I had enough. Together we wrote down the recipe in Bahasa Tabulahan and at the same time I was mixing the bread and had her reading out the Tabulahan version of the bread recipe we had typed up. Isaac was a big distraction by now and Fraser was wanting to start school, so while she wrote out the recipe again and started orthography testing with Robin, I started Fraser (and Isaac) on the day's lessons.*

*While all this was happening, an invitation came to attend a PKK\* event in which the ladies of the area had prepared food of nutritional value and learnt new recipes, and they had a little competition going as to who had prepared the best table. The invitation was for 1 o'clock*

---

\* Pemberdayaan Kesejahteraan Keluarga (Family Welfare Empowerment) *and I knew Isaac would not last the distance and I hoped the bread would be baked on time. I had also prepared more than usual because the ladies from across the valley in Tabulahan were to be coming to visit Tanta upstairs this afternoon as well and I wanted to contribute to that in some way. Well, to cut the story short, we made it all—the PKK thing and got back in time (2 kms walk back up the hill) to serve out the bread and chat with friends from Tabulahan. Most had not seen our little house and when they were about to leave, they came down in droves it seemed and asked for worm and cough medicine, iodine tablets, aspirin and eye drops. It was lovely to oblige, although I didn't have any of the empty tins everyone appreciates, and I think I sent most away happy. It is so nice to have an idea of what is valued to bring in as gifts to give out like this. Earlier I would have felt an incredible sense of being taken advantage of, but now I just feel content to give out what we can and feel okay about turning down a request I can't meet or one that is going to deplete supplies unreasonably. But that is rare, and most requests are not at all unreasonable. It means a lot to understand social cues much more.*

It was indeed good to have a better awareness of appropriate gifts to give in a culture where gifts were important and reciprocity a firmly held value. Each time we visited any household we were given a drink of coffee—black and very sweet if they could afford sugar; bitter if they could not. And often there was an invitation to stay for a meal. When new visitors first called at a house there was a tradition of giving each of the visiting children a live chicken, if the host could afford it, an egg each if not. Apparently, the rationale for this was that it would be a shame for the child or children to cry on the way home after visiting, and something warm to hold would keep them happy. Our children ended up with quite a flock of chooks, which we gave to our host family to be reared with theirs.

We tried to be generous, but it was hard to keep up with local generosity. If we gave an article of clothing, there would often be produce brought a day or two later. One family we visited was using an old reed mat as a blanket. We had an extra sheet we weren't using and passed it on to them. Before a week had gone by, two of the daughters dropped in with a couple of litres of coffee beans, a similar amount of rice and a pile of green vegetables.

Our boys were growing fast, and we often had a few items of clothing that would no longer fit them, and there were sometimes items of our own clothing we no longer wore. We brought such clothes to the village expressly for the purpose of leaving them for village families. After a few times when the recipients gave beyond their means, we found that the best timing was to drop the whole bag off at an elder's house as we were leaving the village and ask that the clothes be distributed among the congregation. Up in Langsa', Mariones devised the fairest distribution system, numbering the items and getting people to draw numbers out of a bag. If the clothing item was not suitable for any member of their household, they could then swap it with someone else, or use it as wages for a worker. Even simple things like empty tins were appreciated, so we made sure that the powdered milk and other products we bought in the city were in containers that could be resealed and have a second life in someone else's kitchen. But it was basic medicines that most of our friends sought, and for simple problems these were a help.

Our hostess upstairs continued in her suffering, with many folk coming to visit. The health worker from Sodangan was back in the area and he came a couple of times to prick her swollen feet in a bid to drain them of excess fluid. That made them even sorer and they continued to be swollen. Little baby Elia became very sick with a bad fever at the same time and, just as for his adoptive grandmother, he was given every kind of local care. We prayed, his grandfather prayed, an auntie from down the hill boiled a stone in water, anointed his head, feet, and chest with it and spat some of it into his mouth. And after we gave him some liquid paracetamol his fever came down and he recovered. Mama Ondong's father-in-law was also sick at that time at his home down in the hamlet of Sohongang. Added to his own ill health he was grieving the loss of his wife and his son, both of whom had died within the previous year or so. He claimed to have had visitations from both of them. We were able to get a message through to Ujung Pandang on our hit and miss radio to call his granddaughter/adopted daughter to come urgently. She arrived a day or two before he died. All this sickness and suffering raised questions for us. Why are we not seeing people healed? How should we best pray? How should we react to the families of the sick turning to traditional beliefs and practices? What do we really desire to happen here?

Delwyn wrote:

> *Tonight, we listened to [our home church pastor] Murray's message on the call to Abraham to 'bless the peoples of the earth' and we were encouraged afresh in our task here. I keep thinking though how important it is that we have the compassion of the Lord. Jesus had a beautiful tender heart to those in need and yet spoke with rebuke to those who needed it too. I think of how much more I would pray and seek the Lord for the people here if I could have His compassion... There are two things I long for right now: Firstly, a longing to bring glory to the Lord in what we do here and not chalk up experiences that will glorify us. Secondly,*

*a true compassion that will bring me to my knees in prayer in a way I've never known before. Maybe then we will see the Lord move on the deaf and the blind here and pour out His Spirit such that they will put complete trust in Him and not keep turning to old beliefs in times of crisis.*

The 'auntie' from the village of animists visited a couple more times to continue her treatment on our hostess. Curiosity also brought her down to our little dwelling underneath the house, though she would not cross the threshold, choosing rather to sit on the floor in the doorway. She had two acolytes with her—teenage girls whom she was training up in the ways of shamanistic practice. She would not allow them to enter either. We boiled up some water to make a drink for them. Most of our guests enjoyed the hot chocolate we had brought from the city, but when this guest realised it contained milk, one of her taboos, she prevented the two young assistants from drinking it. And, as for her own cup, she dipped her finger into it and put it to her lips before taking her leave. This was her way of keeping to her taboo, while meeting both social protocol and superstitions, where to refuse a drink would have been bad luck as well as impolite. Tanta upstairs had good and bad days, but her legs remained swollen and seemed worse, if anything, after fluid was 'drained'.

This trip was a short one, compared to some of the earlier ones, but it was very productive in advancing our language goals and one or two linguistic questions were answered. With the grammar workshop coming up in Ujung Pandang, this was especially pleasing for me. There was a lot to be thankful for. We had kept in good health apart from two kinds of worms. The radio, though erratic was working sufficiently well for us to briefly communicate. We had wonderful times of visiting households and hosting guests in our own place.

Delwyn too seemed more at peace, despite the surrounding sickness, and we both felt we were where we were meant to be. Delwyn had an established, though highly interruptible, routine that included a time after the boys were in bed when she could read by the tiny kerosene lamp and pray. She wrote:

*I have to say that this trip has done much for my spiritual dryness and the Lord has filled my heart with joy and a new song.\**

Delwyn would sing her new songs, along with older ones, while sitting under a rice barn in her morning quiet time. She sang when she was doing the laundry or bathing in a corner of the rice field at the back of the house. And on the occasions when she joined the ladies for a day of harvesting rice, she was repeatedly asked to sing. "We don't get tired," they told her, "when there is something to listen to." It was a satisfying feeling to have at the end of the day to know she had put in a full shift, though with far fewer bundles tied than those of her co-workers. Then, with itchy legs from stubble scratches and leech bites, she would take her song-drained sore throat home.

I came down with fever, chills, dizziness and a terrible headache two days before we were to leave the area. We were down in Tabulahan at the time, and I was too weak to carry Isaac back up the hill, so Delwyn had to and found out just how heavy our two-year-old had become. On reaching Salu Leäng I took some paracetamol and went to bed. When I awoke in the evening my headache was worse than ever and my fever had not gone down at all. I was shivering uncontrollably. Suspecting malaria, I dosed myself with chloroquine and went back to bed.

\* See song: 'Bless the Lord, My Soul'

The following day I was much improved, which was just as well as it was packing up day. Packing up day was simpler when we first began work in the area, and also in later years when we came less often and had no dwelling place of our own. At this point, however, it took quite a slice of the day before we left. In addition to getting our bits and pieces together that we would be taking out with us, including two-way radio and computer, and arranging for the hiring of any horses needed, this involved packing up the house itself. The main aspects of this were putting all kitchenware and non-perishable foodstuffs into the rat-proof wooden boxes that doubled as our kitchen seating (more rat-retardant than rat-proof), bundling up our bedding and mosquito nets to be stored in the rat-retardant cupboard, and rolling and suspending our kapok mattresses from the ceiling in order to deter rats from eating them. That done we would sleep upstairs in one of the rooms of our host family and pray for, among other things, a good trip out, with dry weather an extra blessing.

It took us a record two and a half days to get back to Ujung Pandang that trip, with perfect overcast but dry weather and a good horse for Fraser to ride on among the bags when the trail was not too steep. And on arrival at Mambi it was still early enough in the day to keep going. The car started first time and we were soon on our way. We overnighted in Polewali, reaching the big city at lunch time on the third day. Thank You, Lord!

## 11

# Writing Competition

Although we mostly loved our times in the village and knew it to be the best possible place for learning the Tabulahan language, it was not the best place for writing academic papers to fulfil our obligations with our organisation and university sponsors. There was no electricity supply in the village, and our primitive little laptop could only be used for about three hours a day with the solar charging it received. So, there were times when we spent two or three months in the city. Often there was a seminar or workshop to attend. Often there was paperwork needing attention: several days taken up with driver's licence renewal or car registration, visa renewals, re-entry permits or applying for documents for travel within Sulawesi. And sometimes it was just more convenient to be at our rented home in Palu where we had a consistent power supply, and the computer could be used from daybreak to late evening.

After the grammar workshop in Ujung Pandang, we had a program planning meeting there to get direction on what our next steps should be in advancing our learning and meeting academic expectations. First, I needed to finish off my phonology paper with recommendations for the expected orthography. Second, I needed to get a grammar paper ready to publish. Then Delwyn needed to write a sociolinguistic study on Tabulahan society. Also, the conversations we had been gathering needed to be formatted to become a trilingual conversation book and printed to be the first written materials available in the language. I had another grammar paper that I should be working towards, and the dictionary database needed further work. And we were meant to be getting a portfolio of photos, maps and general info together to hand in to our sponsors. By April. And we were planning on heading back to the village in February. Christmas would be brief.

In fact, we had a lovely Christmas. Our friends Don and Shari worked in a language allocation in the mountains near Palu and they kindly invited us to spend Christmas with them there. Their home had that rustic charm of something between a log cabin and an old-fashioned Kiwi 'bach'. And, at 4,000 feet, the air was cool enough to imagine we were back in a New Zealand Christmas climate—of course not quite cool enough for a European or American Christmas!

Then in early January Delwyn's mother came to stay with us, bringing a second Christmas in the form of some of the items we had largely missed for the past four years: Vegemite, Weetbix and homemade marmalade. She had volunteered to help with the children's program at the conference to be held near Ujung Pandang at the end of the month. We decided to drive down with her via Tanah Toraja, so she could see the tourist hub of Sulawesi en route to the conference. From there we would be able to see her off at the airport before we headed north to the village.

Lia was a university student from Tanah Toraja who lived with us in our house in town and did domestic duties for a wage. A few days before we were to leave Palu, Lia heard news that her father had died suddenly in her home town in Tanah Toraja. She went ahead of us on a bus, but we were there in time to sit with her and her family as they mourned around the large, decorated coffin in the front room. The following day we attended the funeral. Her father was interred in a burial site within the town confines. Funerals in Tanah Toraja can be very elaborate—sometimes burying the deceased high in cliffside tombs outside the villages, often two or three years after the death in order to accumulate a sufficient number of buffalos to feed mourners over a protracted period. This, by contrast, was a very moderate funeral with only two buffalos killed, but still far more elaborate than any funeral we ever witnessed in Tabulahan.

The annual program conference was something we always looked forward to. It was a time of spiritual refreshing and mutual encouragement as well as of meetings and planning. At that time there were sixteen families and one single woman each working in a different language of Sulawesi, along with several other families and singles working in the city as support personnel in administrative, academic, I.T., children's education and library roles. Once a year we all got together and discovered what others had found encouraging or challenging and how best to be praying for them. It was also a time of fellowship around a game of volleyball, ultimate frisbee or a paperchase in the sweltering heat or in an ankle-deep deluge, and in the evening around a hilarious game of Pictionary: guys against girls. And the food was the best of local fare. I couldn't get enough of it.

On the way to the village following conference, we stopped at Polewali as usual to change wheels and report to government offices. There was a new head in the socio-political department who scrutinised our paperwork more than usual and noted that Delwyn's and the boys' names had not been written on the letter from Ujung Pandang. He wanted us to drive back several hours to the city to get a new travel document. In the end he relented and allowed us to continue, stressing that the error was entirely our fault for not having checked it before we left. We thanked the Lord for unexpected lenience and for the good dry weather that kept the road to Mambi easily navigable. Delwyn was suffering from an infected toe that was a concern for the next two days' walk. There were not as many horses available as we needed, so we left most of our stuff there in order that Delwyn could ride on one of them. Some of the time Fraser rode with her when too tired to walk; sometimes Isaac rode when I was getting tired carrying him. At one point on the second day Isaac was fast asleep in front of Delwyn when the horse avoided the narrow path as it went down a decline, choosing rather the flatter verge on the left. By the time his handler redirected it, there was a drop of at least one metre down to the track. Surprisingly, he did not get Delwyn and Isaac to dismount first, and the horse and Delwyn had a jarring landing back on the track. Isaac continued his sleep, blissfully unaware of the drop.

Once back in the village there was more grief. Two of our extended family were missing. Little baby Elia had always been tiny and frail. We had hoped that his recovery from a near-death fever four months back was the beginning of better things. But while we were away, he developed another fever and died a day or so later. It hit us even harder that our dear hostess and 'Tanta', Indo Datu, succumbed to her heart condition before Christmas. The household seemed sombre without her. And we found ourselves weary and sad for much of that trip. Within a few days after our arrival, we went across to the ridge below Langsa' where she, Elia and other family members had been buried. We both shed a tear, remembering Tanta's uncomplicated gentleness and remarked that we had forgotten her Christian name was Esther, a name we had always liked and thought we might call our daughter if God ever chose to bless us with one.

That same day there was a funeral for Ambe Ale', the Kombeng patriarch who had shown us the traditional two-stringed instrument on a previous trip. His eldest son lived in Palu and had given us some early lessons in speaking Tabulahan before we had official permission to begin the project. Soon after we arrived and had visited his sick father, we sent a message via the radio for him to come. It was a day or two after the funeral that he arrived.

Delwyn summed up our mood:

*The death and sickness, poverty and number of people not here for one reason or another is quite depressing, and I've felt so weary with it all. I just feel like crying all the time and I find walking around the area more tiring than usual... I'm amazed at how uptight and weary I have felt. My struggle with homesickness and the uncertainty of the [government] contract have caused a frequent knot in my stomach. I've tried (and many times it does make a difference) to praise and thank the Lord for His love and pray for strength to carry on.*

He did give us strength, and, despite the discouraging days, there were plenty of positive days too. There was a wedding—and weddings were always a good day of celebration: walking with the groom's party to the bride's house, accompanied by the music of a bamboo band. Thence to the church as a larger party and then on to the reception at someone's house. So, plenty of interaction on the trail and around a meal of meat and rice. One day we decided to visit Mama and Papa Tahe' across in Tabulahan and stay the night there. It was a really good visit, reaffirming our friendship and showing that we had not abandoned them as a cherished host family when we moved up to Salu Leäng. The boys played happily with Yahya and So'yang, two of their sons, while we had some meaningful conversations with their parents on several topics.

Delwyn continued in her various roles including homeschooling Fraser. This was no easy task in the early days when he would far rather be outside climbing trees, catching fish or helping to feed chickens or move a buffalo than indoors writing a sentence or two or, worst of all, painting a picture! But he was wonderfully outgoing, interested in what everyone he met was doing. He amazed everyone at his language ability. He even gave some of his friends English lessons, orally translating story books into Tabulahan for onlookers as he read to his brother. Isaac played outside happily most of the time unless Fraser's schoolwork involved using scissors, when he would try to cut up everything in sight. It was at this point that he discovered that most useful of words: 'because'. And this magic word became his reason for everything. No other explanation was necessary.

I can't remember now what first prompted it, but during this trip we discussed with Mariones and others the possibility and logistics of holding a writing competition. We had largely nailed down what the orthography should be, but I was interested to see how folk attempted to write down their language when they had only ever written in the national language previously. A second plus would be that we would receive a large body of texts for future analysis of the language. And a third benefit could be that the best of the entries could be published as reading materials in a bid to promote vernacular literacy among the villagers. There was even a fourth good reason to do this. Few in the area had sufficient clothing. We could offer a free t-shirt to everyone who entered, without then being inundated by coffee and vegetables in payment.

I drafted a letter to be read out in the church notices and Delwyn wrote copies of this for each of the congregations. Writers could choose from any of four genres: (1) narrative—either traditional folk tales or Bible stories retold in their own words, (2) procedural (detailing a process, e.g., a favourite recipe, or how to construct a rice barn), (3) hortatory (encouraging a certain course of action), (4) expository (explaining something). In fact, we would gratefully receive any texts of any other genre too but wanted to give some options to encourage diversity. There was also to be a three-way age distinction: children, young adults and older folk. Everyone who entered would get a t-shirt and there would be three prizes for each age group.

On the following Sunday these letters were read out in each of the congregations and there was a buzz of discussion following the services. Some were sceptical, thinking, "I'll believe it when I see it." Others were keen to get started right away. Up in Langsa' Mariones confirmed to all she met that it was not a hoax—that indeed there would be a t-shirt for everyone who entered—and encouraged everyone to write something. There was plenty of time to decide what to write—the judging of the competition was to be held in six weeks' time—but all who were interested needed to register before we left the village so we could get the requisite number of t-shirts printed. By the time we headed back to the city there were 240 people registered. Fortunately, buying blank t-shirts and getting them screen printed turned out to be considerably cheaper in Indonesia than back home.

Although it would be weeks before the judging took place, some keen writers got started straight away. And the process produced a lot of discussion. "Where is it best to make the word breaks?" "Is this one word or two?" "What do you use for the [æ] sound?" "How about the glottal stop sound?" There were children who wanted to make sure they used correct terms that older folk would approve of, rather than imported slang, and such dialogued with their grandparents to that end. There were grandparents who had little or no literacy but who could spin a good yarn, and some of these directed younger family members to write down their entry. And in between there were others who were capable writers of Indonesian who found the task a little tricky, but not impossible. Among these there were some excellent entries in various genres. There were also educated members of the community who could have put in entries but chose not to. One of these, a school teacher, tried to buy one of the t-shirts with a bunch of bananas despite not having written anything. By far the most entries were narrative texts: mostly old folktales, but with a good smattering of retold Bible stories among them. These, I figured, would be a possible starting point for certain terms used when it came to beginning Scripture translation.

Along with Mariones, we set about thinking what would be good to write on the t-shirts. Our first thought was the (yet to be translated) verse John 14:6, *"Jesus answered, 'I am the way and the truth and the life. No one comes to the Father except through me.'"* We later heard that this was one Bible verse not allowed to be broadcast on national media. "And," we were advised, "other verses may also be controversial on such public billboards as t-shirts. Better stick to something generic." We thought some more and decided that the most appropriate thing would be something relevant to the competition and its goal of increasing vernacular literacy. In the end we went for (the Tabulahan version of) "I am glad that I can write my language, the language of the Tabulahan people."

\*\*\*\*

We spent a few extra days staying in Ujung Pandang following those weeks in the village in order to buy the plain t-shirts and get them screen printed, along with nine sarongs for prizes. The journey from there is etched forever on my memory. With two days of driving ahead, we set out before dawn from the house of our Kiwi friends, Ian and Tania Vail. It was Ramadan, the Muslim fasting month, and we knew many people would be thronging the streets after prayers in their mosques. We hoped to be well clear of the city before daybreak. Not far beyond the city limits traffic slowed as we approached a mosque from which scores of people had just exited. Some of these were spilling into the road enjoying the festive atmosphere before daylight spelled another twelve hours of going without food. We were travelling behind a large van. Suddenly there was a bicycle turning into our path in front of us. The 18-year-old peddler could not see where he was going for the 18-year-old passenger sitting on his handlebars. Assuming he could turn behind the van from his side of the road to ours, he drove straight into our path. I braked hard but the collision was inevitable. The passenger managed to bail before the bike caught our right mudguard. It was still dark, and we couldn't see what had happened to the youths, but we had been told that we should head straight to the nearest police station without stopping should we ever have an accident. The nearest police station was at Maros, a few kilometres ahead.

The duty policeman at the guard post ushered us to the main office. A man in plain clothes was sweeping. I asked if he was a policeman too. "Oh no," said the constable. "He was the driver of a car that killed someone. He is here for his own protection." I went cold at the thought.

I noticed several vehicles in variously damaged states as we walked. "What happened to those?" I asked.

"Oh, they are vehicles that have been in accidents. You see that burned out shell of a van?" I nodded. "That was in an accident and the driver managed to escape by running away. So, the family of the injured person burned his car." I was glad we hadn't stopped.

After a couple of hours of waiting, during which someone

was dispatched to the scene of the accident, we were informed that the police had recovered the bike, but had not yet found the others involved. We were to go back to Ujung Pandang and return at 9:00 a.m. the next day, when all parties would be there. The Vails were very accommodating and put us up again for the night and prayed for us before we left next morning.

Back at the police station we met the mother of one of the youths with her son and the father of the other. The mother had drawn a sketch of her version of events with our vehicle wholly on the wrong side of the road. The duty sergeant sternly pointed out how we had been at fault. I explained to him what had actually happened and drew another sketch. I also explained that I was aware that, as the driver of the more expensive vehicle, I would be expected to pay any damages. He seemed to relax at that. At this point the woman demanded that the bike be repaired, that we should pay for medical costs and loss of pay for her son who couldn't go to work. "I want Rp. 200,000," she said. I looked at the youth who had nothing more than a grazed hand with a bit of gentian violet smeared across it. I told the sergeant that I was happy to pay for any real costs, like the damaged bike, but not imagined ones. He then rebuked the woman for trying to extort money from a foreign guest and ordered a constable to accompany me to a cycle repair shop nearby to get the bike fixed. Half an hour later we were back with the bike in perfect working order. It had cost me a negligible amount.

Meanwhile Delwyn was talking to the father of the other youth, a man about 70 years of age. "I'm sorry we didn't stop to help at the time like we would in our country," she said. "But we had been told to come straight to the police."

"Oh, you did the right thing. I'm glad you did. If you had stopped, I would have killed you." He seemed relieved that we had removed the burden of customary retribution from him.

Besides the bike repair, I also paid a small amount for the gentian violet and, after we had all signed forms saying we would take the matter no further, we were allowed to continue on our way. A constable showed us out to our car. "Why don't you have a driver?" he asked. "If you had a driver and you had an accident, we could lock him up and you could continue on your way."

Leaving so late in the day, we knew we would not reach Pendolo for the night, but made good progress to reach Mangkutana at about 8:00 p.m. The next day we reached a long line of vehicles as we approached the border area between South and Central Sulawesi. I wandered to the front of the line to find out what the holdup was. A man told me that around the next bend there was a huge landslide. He was the driver of one of the trucks that had been waiting there for ten days for it to be cleared. He must have seen my face fall. "Don't worry," he told me. "It will definitely be cleared today."

"How do you know?" I asked.

"Because the Minister of the Interior is scheduled to be coming through tomorrow. It will have to be cleared today."

Ten hours later the road was sufficiently cleared such that trucks and 4WDs could negotiate their way to the head of the landslide, where a bulldozer would tow them through 100 metres of the worst of it. Vans and smaller vehicles were paired with 4WDs or trucks to get them to that point. When it was our turn, we towed a van for a few hundred metres round a couple of switchbacks until we reached the bulldozer. Then we were towed one at a time through what seemed like liquid concrete, half a metre deep. We breathed a collective sigh of relief and thanked the Lord that our minor accident two days before had saved us two nights of sitting in a queue of trucks in the middle of nowhere.

## 12

# The Miry Clay

We had often encountered knee-deep mud on our walks in and out of the village or ended up staring at the sky after a slip on wet clay when walking between hamlets in Salu Leäng. It is hardly surprising that the opening verses of Psalm 40 were a recurrent theme for us, especially after the last trip back to Palu.

> *I waited patiently for the Lord; he turned to me and heard my cry. He lifted me out of the slimy pit, out of the mud and mire; he set my feet on a rock and gave me a firm place to stand. He put a new song in my mouth, a hymn of praise to our God.* (Psalm 40:1-3a)

Once again, these words were applicable on our next trip, and once again hundreds of kilometres from the village. We had an extra passenger this trip. Lia was about to head home for a break. Rather than catching a bus to Tanah Toraja, we suggested she travel with us the next day. It was not far out of our way.

With provisions for the coming weeks, and with 240 t-shirts neatly printed and individually packaged in plastic bags, we set out once more from Palu. We had also purchased a few sarongs as prizes for winners of the various categories of the writing contest. These most useful of garments were universally treasured. Anyone could always use a second or third. Apart from their standard usage as wrap-around skirts and bottomless sleeping bags, they are often worn as shawls in cool weather, as head coverings when working outside, or as head cushioning under a bamboo conical hat; as belts, more to hold a small rolled-up package than to keep trousers up; as baby slings, with baby in front, round the back or hanging in the swing the sarong has become when suspended from a hook. We have seen them used as umbrellas, as firewood bundle ties, as rucksacks. And then there is that most ingenious of uses: as a wall to lean on, whereby a person sitting on the floor in a room where the only space is in the middle sits inside the sarong and braces his feet against the side opposite. He can sit this way for hours without fear of backache.

We had heard that the road through the border area was open, so expected no delays and made good time through Central Sulawesi to Pendolo at the southern end of Lake Poso. It was about 4 o'clock when we reached there, so decided to press on to Mangkutana in South Sulawesi for the night. Half an hour later we rounded a corner and joined a line of several vehicles vainly trying to negotiate a section of road partially buried in a landslide. Two trucks were firmly stuck at the front of the queue. Rain was also beginning to set in, so we turned around and sought shelter and a night's rest at Pendolo.

The following morning we returned to the border area only to find the situation worse. There had been another landslide during the night which had half buried one of the now *three* stuck trucks! On the bright side, this had prevented the new landslide from completely obliterating the road. Beyond this the truck at the far end was over towards the left, so any passing would have to be through the deeper mud. In front of us there were three 4WDs and another truck, followed by two vans. We seriously considered returning to Palu to fly from there and then take public transport. Of course, this would not help Lia. We decided to wait a while in the hope that help would arrive. This was unlikely given that the road crews with their bulldozers and graders had all gone home for the *Idul Fitri* celebrations.

In the meantime, we videoed the scene while Lia stayed with the boys. By combining forces, towing each other and pushing, the three 4WDs managed to carve a track through the quagmire and continued on their way. Before anyone could stop him, the driver of the next truck ploughed in and got well and truly stuck next to the number three stuck truck. For the next two hours everyone was pitching in, digging and pushing, with our Land Cruiser towing in a bid to get this truck back to where it started. Otherwise, no one would be able to get through from either direction. We set a time limit of 9:30. If there was no improvement, we would return to Palu.

Right on 9:30 the truck moved back a metre, then some more, and soon we had it back out of the way. At the same time a 4WD reached the far end of the landslide from the south, so we knew there was a through road up ahead. The van drivers were willing to let us go next, given that we had 4WD, but understandably they also requested that we tow them as we went. I was not sure we would get through without any extra drag but conceded that I might try towing one of them. For the next two hours we made slow progress with many stops, reversals, pushes and leverages, until finally we rounded the last truck with both of us through. Unfortunately, the angle of rounding one of the trucks while towing had caused a long gash in one of our side panels, but at least we were on the other side and able to carry on our way.

A couple of days later Delwyn's journal expressed our feelings:

*I never knew one could shake with relief, but I just wanted to cry all the way down to Mangkutana, and when we stopped to eat 1 ½ hours later I dropped a plate someone had passed me—my nerves still felt shot. I guess I was so grateful we weren't heading back to Palu to try to get a flight to Ujung Pandang and then go carless to the village. Again Psalm 40 was a blessing. I was quoting the first verse to Robin on the journey to the border that morning, and the 'waiting patiently' bit turned out so exact, not to mention 'the mud and mire'. It was almost like crossing the Red Sea, I reckon. 'My heart fails within me' was how I felt when there was little hope. It was a dreadful draining feeling. 'Many, O Lord my God, are the wonders You have done' has become my new song and very much the theme of the week.* \*

The Lord's timing is always perfect, although it doesn't often quite line up with our own schedule. The extra time spent on the road and dropping Lia off in Tanah Toraja had only put us a day behind, but we were still keen to get to the village without further delay. On the Mambi road we met Gerson going the other way. He usually arranged horses for us from Mambi, but wouldn't be there to do so. His suggestion was to send word to Aralle from Mambi for someone to come from there with horses. We did so, hoping they would not only come but would get there good and early so that we could set out before the day got too hot. It was already warm by 8 o'clock in the morning and by 8:30 we were getting restless and impatient. "If they don't come by 9 o'clock there is no point going today!" Delwyn said. "We'll be walking through the heat of the day and not get to Taora until it's dark, like that

---

\* See song: 'Many are the Wonders'

*The Miry Clay*

first trip." At 9:00 on the dot the horses arrived and, shortly after, the bags were in place, and we set off with a mixture of gratitude and grumbling. By mid-afternoon we could see that there was heavy rain up ahead on the Taora hill. But by the time we started the climb the rain had stopped. The steep slope had not retained much of it and we arrived at Taora on a dry path and before dark. If the horses had come when we wanted them to, we would have been caught in the rain and had soggy clothing to set out in next day. Oh, we of little trust!

The Aralle horsemen had never been farther inland than Taora and were not keen to take us further on our way. So, we left 90 percent of our stuff, including all the competition t-shirts and sarongs, and set off by ourselves. Once we reached Salu Bahka' we found a couple of young guys keen to earn a bit of money by carrying Fraser and Isaac the rest of the way. They set such a cracking pace that we reached Salu Leäng by 3:30, giving us time to sweep out and set up the house that day, rather than the day after arrival as was usual. In effect that had put us completely back on schedule! "Thank You, Lord! And sorry about the grumbling."

The next few days were busy gathering competition entries from various villages and sorting them into their relevant categories based on age of writer and genre chosen. Although many were completed by this time, others trickled in over the next couple of weeks. We decided that we should not be the ones to judge the competition—we might have had a good idea of appropriate orthography considerations, but we could not judge what was considered to be the best retelling of a story we had never heard before. And rather than select judges who had expressed no interest in the competition, we thought it appropriate to choose judges from among those who had entered, provided that they were only judging categories other than their own.

Delwyn continued to work with Mariones on Friday afternoons and was planning to begin to translate the story of Joseph in Genesis with her. As yet I had still found no one to work with me regularly on translation, but I had had some good sessions with Pa' Pandita thinking through key terms that we would need later when translating the New Testament—terms like: Messiah, Kingdom of God, baptise, repentance, faith, Sanhedrin, Temple, altar, Holy of Holies, Tabernacle.

In between, there were the usual visits, calling in on neighbours for a chat, as well as the sick, or anyone else who called us in as we passed by. Each of these visits helped build bonds with the community and increased our fluency in the language. Tuesdays were market days. There was a circuit of markets around the wider area, each on a different day. For Tabulahan this was Tuesday. There were usually some consumables that we were running low on: kerosene, soap, batteries, sardines or noodles, for example. Even if our stocks were good, we generally went across the valley on a Tuesday morning to socialise with folk we only ever saw in the marketplace. And on the way home there would always be at least one house we were passing when we were called out to. "Stop by! Rest first!" And we usually would. There was always a cup of coffee brought out for us, often with some kind of snack, usually bananas. Often, we were called out to from several houses. I remember stopping in at six places on the way back from market one day, each serving us black coffee and a plate of bananas. We arrived home mid-afternoon very full and slightly hyper.

We too were about to host visitors. Our program director, Ron, had been concerned about the branch director, Jim. He had been under a huge amount of pressure in Jakarta, trying to work out new agreements with other government departments following the Department of Education and Culture's

*The Miry Clay*

decision to not renew our contract. Ron thought it would be good for him and his wife, Peggy, to have a break from the office in the form of a trip to visit three village teams in Sulawesi. They had visited the Mattis in Mamasa and the Campbells in Bambam and were now on their way from Mambi to visit us. Ron had been to Tabulahan twice before, but not through Mambi. For his wife, Esther, and their elder son, Micah, this would be a first trip into the area, as it would for Jim and Peggy. We prayed that it would not be too arduous a trip for them and that they would indeed get the rest and refreshing they needed. Delwyn was a little anxious about hosting folk, some of whom we had never met before, and particularly guests from America. Our meals were pretty basic village fare.

They arrived at 4:30 on Friday afternoon, Peggy on horseback, the others walking. They all looked glad to have reached their destination, but tired—apart from Ron, always the comic. "What? We're here already? I can't believe we are already here." Delwyn need not have worried—our five North American visitors were all very gracious, having some of everything we served up to them. (I wouldn't be surprised, though, if Ron and Micah supplemented their diet by eating Snickers bars in bed later.) They were only planning to be there two nights, but we managed to persuade them to stay an extra night so as not to be too tired before they set out again. We went with them on some short wanders around rice fields and up to Langsa' to visit some of our friends up there. In the evenings Ron and Esther introduced us to Nertz, a frantic card-slapping game, not unlike Dutch Blitz. It was a fun time with a lot of laughs. Only Jim was quiet.

On the Sunday afternoon we went for a walk along the rice terraces near the house to enjoy the last of the sun. It was one of those magic afternoons, in which a thick cloud has darkened the sky to the east and the low sun is bathing everything with a floodlight of gold.* There was also a vivid rainbow arching high over Mt Tatondong, followed by a rich red sunset over the fading layers of ridges to the west. It was a 'Wow, God!' moment. That evening we had a heart-felt prayer time together and Jim began to talk. We felt the Lord had provided the sunset just for him.

After our guests left, a busy couple of weeks ensued in which we distributed competition entries to judges in various villages, then a week later retrieved them along with the results. Sometimes this necessitated a second or third trip. After that there were trips to take bundles of t-shirts to each congregation leader for distribution, along with the results to be read out and one or more sarongs if any of that flock had won one of the competition's categories.

Delwyn and Mariones began a first draft of the story of Joseph while I was still struggling to find suitable men to work with me. Yunus, one I thought had all the requisite qualities, agreed to come, and after a couple of days of not showing up, came one day and we managed to make a start on a few verses from Mark's Gospel. The next day he returned, but as soon as we had prayed and were about to reopen the Word, an unexpected guest arrived—an official from the immigration department in Pare-Pare, three hours north of Ujung Pandang. He was keen to ask us a lot of questions and take our photograph and he insisted that we needed to be registered with immigration in Pare-Pare. We protested that we were in fact resident in Palu and were therefore registered with immigration there. In the end we promised to check with our Jakarta

---

* In Tabulahan, we call this *allo koro* 'monkey sun', because in this light monkeys are sometimes seen coming out of the forest to raid gardens.

office for advice. He stayed with us, plying us with questions until after lunch, by which time we had killed a chicken to feed him. He was the only Indonesian official ever to visit us in the village. Our efforts to make a solid start on translation were thwarted for the day, as Yunus had to return home after lunch. And he found that he was busy each day thereafter. I continued my search.

There was one person whom I was keen not to work with. I had heard him using some awful language towards someone and there were rumours about him being involved with a woman other than his wife. Despite not being invited to, he aggressively informed me with a steely stare that he was going to work with me on translation. This was something I never agreed to, but that did not stop him showing up anyway. Instead, I had invited Bo'o to work with me. He was a humble young man and intelligent, hampered only by being slightly deaf. During our first session we spent the morning going over translation principles, rather than launching into translating any verses. Just before lunch, after which Bo'o and I would be working on translation, the aggressive man showed up. Delwyn and I both felt that here again was an unsubtle attempt by the enemy to thwart the translation process.

For most of the afternoon he hung around and came back into our house to see what we were up to, even sitting alongside Bo'o and me to listen to what we were discussing. The Lord gave both Delwyn and me a peace about the situation, whereas we had been uptight around this person on more than one occasion in the past. In the end he left, and Bo'o and I managed to translate six verses from Mark. Bo'o agreed to work with me the next morning and Yunus had said he could come in the afternoon. Neither came. We discussed and prayed about the situation. The story of Nehemiah was encouraging—how the Lord opened the way for him to begin the work, rather than him forcing it. Maybe we had got the timing wrong, or perhaps had approached the wrong people. There was a possibility that Mariones could come to Palu with us for a few weeks when we left the village and there she might be able to work with both of us on translation.

A couple of weeks later the writing competition was all wrapped up. All the entrants had received their t-shirts, the winners had also received their sarongs and we had 240 pieces of writing to wade through, using the best for analysis and future publications. Best of all, some people who were barely literate now realised that it was possible to write in their own language which they spoke fluently, rather than in the national language in which they had a very limited vocabulary. One such was Tura. She had had very little schooling and had been assisting Delwyn with some domestic chores in the village. With encouragement from Mariones, Tura had put in a short entry for the competition. It was not a winner, but she was. As well as a t-shirt, she had gained the self-confidence to give writing a go. A few days later when we were out for the morning, we came home to find a simple note written by Tura in her own language. That was a first and we were so encouraged.

When it was time to head back to Palu, both Mariones and Tura came with us for a month, at the end of which Delwyn recorded:

*What a contrast today compared to the previous entry! We've just had over three weeks with Mariones (and Tura) in Palu majoring in translation. She has finished drafting the Joseph story and I'm just checking the last few chapters with her. Robin has completed translating the healing miracles in Mark with her. What an answer to prayer she has been and under our noses all the time!*

*Tonight, we just had a tremendous talk about a number*

*of things as we checked the translation. We talked about curses, and I found out that many Tabulahan people use curses and feel they are bound by them. We talked about being Christian and not tied to a particular denomination. We talked about how to memorise Scripture and meditate on it, asking the Lord to reveal His ways. We talked about the opposition of Satan and the victory in Christ, the power of intercession and how God can call on a person to pray for us.*

*For the first time I feel I have found someone here I can invest in who has an open heart to hear and carefully evaluate what I say, who truly wants to follow the Lord and who has a vision for the power of the translated Word. It has been such a busy month with many and varied pressures, but I feel this is the jewel we have been looking for, and the Lord is encouraging us at a time when we feel so tired. It feels so neat to be able to encourage her and stir her faith and to have had this time in our home to develop a firm friendship. I feel she will be able to draft some while we are on furlough with the training she has had now. Praise the Lord! His purposes will be established!*

There was time for just one more short trip to the village before our first furlough. We needed to take Mariones and Tura back and there were a few loose ends to deal with. It turned out to be our longest journey to or from Tabulahan—seven days. This was not due to road conditions—the Trans-Sulawesi Highway was good and clear again, apart from a short three and a half hour wait for some road works. Rather, there was an extra overnight at Mamasa, which became our new location for the car's mud wheels, and an unexpected delay at Mambi. We were ready to set out, just putting on our sunscreen for the hike to Taora, when we heard that the horses had run away and that it would be afternoon by the time they were rounded up. We chose to drive back down the road to see the Campbells and spent the night with them in their village home. Two days later in Taora, Isaac fell down a ladder, cutting his head quite badly. Then Fraser came down with sharp abdominal pains once we reached Salu Leäng. We feared appendicitis and thought we might have to turn right around and head out again, but after praying about it decided we should start him on a course of antibiotics. He improved over the next couple of days.

News had got around that we were going to be leaving for a year. Friends dropped by to wish us well, some with gifts to send us on our way, others requesting various items we might not be needing any more. We were indeed trying to whittle down some things, but we could not meet all these requests without having to completely set up house again on our return. But would we be returning? The contract situation was still very unclear. It was likely that there would be some visas available through new government departments, but nowhere near as many as previously. Would ours be among them? We didn't know and ended up giving away many of our household items.

The most memorable day during that last two weeks was spent in the rice fields belonging to Mama Ri'na. She invited us up to her *bangsuli*, her field shelter, to share in the meal she was to be preparing for her workers. We decided to go early and work for our meal: Delwyn joined the women to plant the rice seedlings individually that others were pulling up in clumps from their germination bed, while I joined the men to push grassy sods beneath the mud with our feet and to scrape the sides of the dikes with spades. Fraser and Isaac watched on from the dikes, supervised along with other youngsters by one of the older women. We were able to get some good video shots of the process and the communal meal in the shelter and had a wonderful time of conversation with our village friends. It was a day to treasure.

As the time of leaving approached, we began to have apprehensions about furlough. Delwyn often felt some anxiety a day before travel, especially into or out of the village, but this was different. We had been away so long, how would we cope with being back in New Zealand? We had had some cold nights in the village lately, down maybe as far as 18°C. We had shivered. How would we survive the cold of a New Zealand winter? Thankfully, we would be getting home in early spring. What else would be hard to handle? Conversation? This was plainly in our subconscious thought as both of us had dreams of being in New Zealand and not being able to communicate—no one would be able to speak Indonesian or Tabulahan! Our dreams had forgotten about English. But Delwyn was also experiencing the tension of it all physically.

> *I confess I'm still counting the days till we leave. Our weariness is pretty deep – maybe more than we realise. I've had some pre-trip blues with weariness and a heaviness in my chest. Fraser keeps asking when we are going. Isaac tells us about what he is going to do in 'Newz Ealand', so I think the boys sense our restlessness too. I woke this morning with chest pains and a real sense of heaviness. It has stayed with me all day and coming back up the hill from the church I was quite out of breath. It's hard to know what's wrong. I'm glad to be getting to the end of all the requests and visiting and visitors, but it worries me that I'll be out of breath tomorrow if this persists. We really are going to miss our friends here, but for now it really is time for a break, and I just thank the Lord that we made it to the end of these two weeks.*

*Songs on the Journey*

We left the car with friends in Ujung Pandang for their use while we were on furlough and flew to Palu. Once back there we set about selling off most of our furniture. Our thought was that if we did get to return to Indonesia long term, we would be based in Ujung Pandang, thus saving a day on our journeys. The few items we opted not to sell were put in storage at the office. We returned the keys of the house to the landlord, whom we had not seen since we paid him for the lease three years before. And then it was time to leave.

It was four years and four months since we had last seen our homeland, a new country for Isaac and one not remembered by Fraser. But in that time, we had had the privilege of many new experiences, of making some wonderful friends, of learning three languages,* and even beginning to translate God's Word into one of those previously unwritten. We had so many reasons to be grateful.**

---

\* Before reaching Indonesia we had spent eight months in Papua New Guinea, where we learned to speak Tok Pisin (Melanesian Pidgin).

\*\* See song: 'So Much To Be Thankful For'

*Photos*

*Early days in Palu (top) and Tabulahan (bottom).*

Top: *The Mambi road on a good day.*
Bottom: *Delwyn's least favourite bridge.*

*Photos*

*Top: Meeting the no-nonsense Papa Tahe'.*
*Bottom: Part of the village of Langsa'.*

Songs on the Journey

Top: Tamonseng, one of the hamlets of Salu Leäng.
Bottom, left to right: Mama Ondong, baby Elia, Indo Datu,
Pa' Pandita and us.

*Photos*

*Top: Harvesting the big rice field at the back of the house.
Bottom: Tahe' and Mama Semeng with their
children/grandchildren.*

*Songs on the Journey*

Top: *Phonetic transcription of new expressions.*
Bottom: *Data entry on our first computer.*

*Photos*

*Top: Recording one of many stories from Mariones' father.
Bottom: Language learning through sharing tasks.*

*Songs on the Journey*

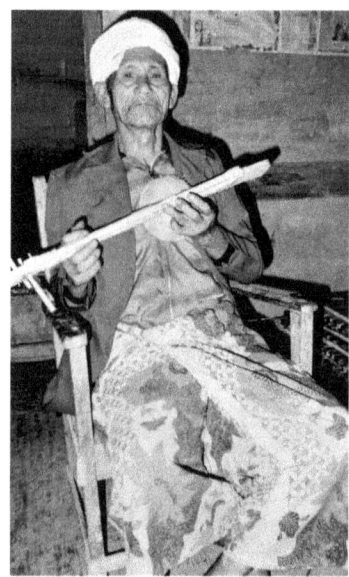
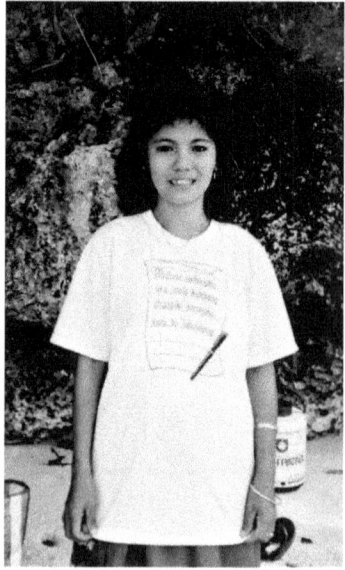

Top: *Orthography testing.*
Bottom, left: *Ambe Alek and his tandilong.*
Right: *Tura sporting her competition t-shirt.*

*Top: Conversation book sparks interest.
Bottom: Distribution of Genesis in one of
the congregations.*

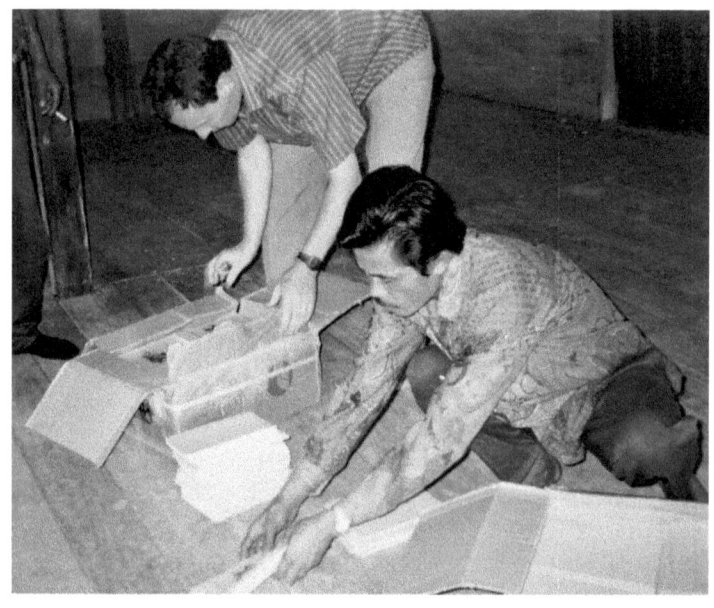

*Top: Unpacking Acts for distribution.*
*Bottom: Indo Bonnäng with her copy of six epistles.*

*Photos*

Top: *Market day in Tabulahan.*
Bottom: *Testing for comprehension.*

Songs on the Journey

Top: Our first apartment in Davao.
Bottom: Recycled crates for homeschooling.

*Photos*

*Top: Rescuing Mum on one of many flood days.*
*Bottom: With translation consultant, Bob Sterner.*

*Top: Delwyn with community orchestra at FAD.*
*Bottom: The woodwork project afloat.*

*Photos*

*Top: Traditional dress for the New Testament dedication.
Bottom: Gathering outside the church for the occasion.*

*Songs on the Journey*

Top, left: Iyä back at work in Lakähäng. Right: Äto' and Uja unboxing the Tabulahan NT.
Bottom, left: Neri, first believer from Aralle, receiving the Word.
Right: Mariones speaking at the NT dedication.

## 13

# New Countries

'Furlough' is a military term for a leave of absence. For many years it has also been applied to missionary service, when an overseas worker finishes a field term and returns to his or her home country for a period of time. This does not mean that the missionary is taking an extended holiday. These days the more accurate term 'home assignment' is generally used.

Within our organisation there has always been an expectation that some sort of group service would be engaged in by the person(s) on home assignment. As part of our time back in New Zealand we were asked to be part of the team teaching a language learning, linguistics and anthropology course at SIL school in Featherston. We had wonderful memories of our own time as students six years earlier, both there and later at Kangaroo Ground on the outskirts of Melbourne.

Apart from teaching, there was a requirement to share about the work of Wycliffe Bible Translators at meetings in various churches, as well as our own part of that work at our supporting churches or anywhere else we were invited to. A theme song for this time and one we shared at several venues sought to remind believers that we are all included in the task.\*

For the rest of our time back in New Zealand we were permitted to continue working on aspects of the Tabulahan

\* See song: 'A Part in Your Plan'

project, whether academic papers, dictionary work or thinking through and making notes on passages to be translated in the future.

In between all this there was an addition to our family. Esther was born at Lincoln Maternity Hospital nine months into our time at home. What a delight to have a daughter as well as two sons. We looked forward to introducing her to all our friends in Indonesia, especially in the villages of Tabulahan, assuming there would be a visa for us to return on.

A sister was not all Fraser and Isaac were getting used to. There were so many weird and wonderful things in this strange land: things like a vacuum cleaner, which the boys kept feeding with items they had found. Then there was the squeeze mop— "Make it clap hands again, Mummy!" And then there was surprise at the ubiquity of toilets— "This house has got a toilet *too*!" In fact, there were things all of us were getting used to, such as the huge variety of items available in a supermarket. On more than one occasion the choices so overwhelmed us that we walked out again without buying the very thing we had gone in for.

And then there was the Kiwi diet. Though we have always loved rice, we ate a lot of potatoes that year. On our first evening we ate fish and chips. We frequently ate meat pies and chips. There was often a Sunday roast on those occasions when we were invited out to someone's house after church. And all those yummy desserts! After a few months we were all looking decidedly pudgy. Towards the end of our time back home some photographs were taken that we refer to as 'the fat family furlough photos'.

We were back home for a year and the months flew past. The time was coming to a close, but still there was no word on a visa to return on. Then one day Wyn Laidig, who had replaced Ron as program director, rang from Ujung Pandang.

He told us that there were no visas forthcoming at that stage for us or for other language projects, but there was a pressing need for someone to take over in Palu as administrator for the Central Sulawesi teams in order to keep things ticking over until the picture became clearer. And hopefully we would be able to do a little language and translation work on the side—like in the evenings. He wanted an immediate commitment to this, but said if we changed our mind, we would have to ring him back within 24 hours. I didn't know what to say. We had all but cut ties with Palu, hoping to be based in Ujung Pandang on our return. On the other hand, would there be any other way to get back? I said, "Yes."

And before we knew it, we were back in Palu.

\*\*\*\*

Our arrival back in Palu coincided with a progressive exodus of our colleagues. As the temporary extensions on their individual visas ran out, they one by one headed back to their home countries for the home assignments they had been putting off. By Christmas we were on our own. Before she too left, Donna Evans was a huge help in getting me up to speed on the various tasks expected of the Palu administrator. I found myself chasing my tail in a bid to get 160 forms filled in for families who were not there and therefore unable to answer my questions in those pre-email days. Computer problems compounded this. I was also spending time on public relations visits to government officials in a vain bid towards future contract negotiations for Central Sulawesi teams. Any hope of getting to the village to contact Tabulahan friends was on hold. We had intended to get one or two of them to come up from the village area and live with us to work with us on the translation. Delwyn, Fraser and young Esther all came down with dengue fever over the Christmas period, at a time when other stresses were pressing in.

The visa we had entered the country with was only a temporary one, so that necessitated trips to the immigration office for monthly extensions. These could be granted in a day. One temporary extension was due to expire on January 3$^{rd}$. Arriving at the immigration office on New Year's Eve, I applied again for an extension. Usually this was processed by office workers in the main office. This time, however, I was called into the office of the head and, for the next hour and a half, was berated for everything he could think of. He flatly refused to give us an extension and said we would have to leave the country. I explained that, as the next three days comprised public holidays and a Sunday, we would not be able to get tickets arranged in order to leave. In the end he agreed to give us a *final* three-week extension, on the proviso that I write a letter promising not to return on any but a long-term visa. I tried to word the letter carefully to avoid committing ourselves to never being able to return to the country, and after sending me home for two rewrites, he eventually accepted it and gave us our extension. I felt drained. Here I was meant to be working toward getting visas for all the Central Sulawesi teams and I couldn't even keep our own visas.

There were four possible neighbouring countries to which we could head for a temporary stay. Of these, Malaysia seemed the best option. There was an SIL group based in Kota Kinabalu, in Sabah. We contacted them and received a warm invitation to join them for however long we needed. Getting there involved two flights after a night sailing on an inter-island passenger ship. We managed to get a second-class cabin on the 'Tidar' from a port near Palu to the Indonesian port of Tarakan. There was no flight to Malaysia that day, so we overnighted at a rather run-down hotel near the port. Next day we heard that, as it was Chinese New Year, there might be no flight to Malaysia that day either. That turned out to be wrong information. There was indeed a flight on a 19-seat Twin Otter, which, though short in duration, gave an interesting view over the meandering rivers and deltas of north Kalimantan.

On arrival at Tawau, it seemed no one was expecting the flight. There were no Malaysian immigration officials at the airport, as everyone was home for Chinese New Year festivities. After a two hour wait, an immigration official turned up to stamp our passports. However, he had no key for the immigration office with him and so could not provide us with entry cards to fill out. Consequently, our passports told us that we were now in Malaysia, but the local authorities had no record that we were in their country. Our last flight took us from Tawau to Kota Kinabalu, where we were met by the SIL director.

Our Malaysia branch colleagues went out of their way to make us feel welcome, organising accommodation, inviting us for meals, even loaning us a car. They were about to hold a six-week grammar workshop and invited me to participate, even though South Sulawesi languages are significantly different from the Philippine-type languages of Sabah. While this was happening, our family was staying at a church campsite several kilometres out of town. It was a lovely rural setting on the edge of a patch of jungle. We often saw large squirrels in the trees, and one day a small python outside the bunkroom. I could catch a couple of buses to and from the city for the grammar workshop each day.

Delwyn's days were not so easy. The bunkroom was very hot and had no power outlets. The kitchen, 25 metres away, was a better place to spend the day, but the floor was rough concrete and not the best for a crawling baby. The toilet/bathroom block was 40 metres the other way, and each of these buildings were inhabited by some of the biggest, meanest rats we ever came across. These would eat any food not secured, any soap left in the bathroom, even biting our toes at night.

There had also been a mix up in the rent we were to pay. Because the fees were calculated daily, rather than as a weekly rental, staying at the campsite turned out to be twice the price of a small apartment in town. When this was discovered, the director found us a tiny, unfurnished apartment and rounded up some basic furnishings from the group. What a contrast—it was just three steps from bedroom to kitchen or to bathroom. It was heaven.

We kept in regular phone contact with our office in Jakarta, hoping for updates on our visa situation. Each time, we were told to sit tight—it was coming. And after two months our Malaysian visa was due to expire, and we had to get a one-month extension on that. We really hoped that our visa to return to Indonesia would be through before that month was up, or we would have to leave Malaysia as well and seek temporary refuge somewhere else.

Before that time elapsed, the Malaysia Branch was to hold a retreat in the foothills surrounding spectacular Mt Kinabalu, followed by their annual conference back in town. They invited us to join them and asked if we would be willing to run the children's program at both locations. That suited us fine. Games and craft activities with a group of lovely children sounded much more fun than sitting through business meetings that were not directly relevant to us. It was a wonderful time of fellowship with new friends, and we were able to get to some of the retreat sessions. Although we wanted to return to Indonesia and continue our work among the Tabulahan people, we enjoyed our time in Malaysia so much that we discussed the possibility of transferring there to begin work on one of the local languages, should we not be able to continue in Tabulahan.

Finally, we were told by our Jakarta office staff to take our passports to the Indonesian Consulate for a visa to be stamped in them. The visa turned out to be the same temporary one that we had been told not to return on. Another quick phone call to Jakarta gave us the advice to return to Palu, stay well away from the immigration office and send our passports to Jakarta to get the promised long-term visa.

On the way out through Tawau there were a few scratched heads, trying to figure out how we could be leaving the country when officially we had not entered. But soon we were back in Indonesia, taking three more flights over a couple of days to get back to Palu. The day we arrived an expatriate friend rang us. "Hi, I don't know if you heard, but, because it is Central Sulawesi Anniversary tomorrow, the immigration office is trying to get all the expats in town to be on their float. Interested?" We declined.

\*\*\*\*

The next few weeks found us in three different locations. First, the biennial branch conference was coming up in Ambon in the Maluku Islands. This, unlike our annual program conference, was a delegate conference. There had been so many members scattered over the archipelago that it was impractical for all members to attend. This year, however, there were so few remaining in the country that both Delwyn and I were delegated to attend. Second, following the conference, we were asked to spend a month in Ujung Pandang to work on the library there. Then, third, we planned to make a very short trip to Tabulahan to see if we could find a couple of girls to help Delwyn in Palu who could also help us with language work.

So, we loaded up the Land Cruiser, ready for the drive to Ujung Pandang, before flying to Ambon. We had only driven 20 kilometres when the engine died, and we had to get towed back home. There was no time to get the car fixed, drive to Ujung Pandang and board our flight for Ambon. If we caught a flight to Ujung Pandang, we could make it, but then we would be without a vehicle for the month there and not so easily able to get to and from the village. I remembered that, before he and his family returned to the United States, our good friends Don and Shari had said we could borrow their car if we needed to. They may have been thinking of its use in the environs of Palu, rather than a two-day road trip each way, but it was exactly what we needed right then. We transferred everything to their Land Cruiser and set off once more.

The conference was a good but sobering time, with so much to discuss about the future potential of the work in Indonesia and possible ways of going about it despite the barriers. Overall, there was a sense that the Lord sees the end from the beginning and has everything under control. From our limited perspective, though, the future looked murky. Delwyn wrote:

> *Our branch director, Larry, shared tonight from Isaiah 6. It was a word for us for this time. He pointed out that Isaiah had willingly said, "Here I am. Send me!" And the message he had to bring was not one of joy and happiness. Yet 'the stumps' that are left of the projects that we may have to leave are in God's hands and He can cause them to grow again in His timing. It affected Robin and me deeply as we look at the possible ending of our project in Tabulahan. I still can't believe that it is the end, but at this stage it looks pretty grim and doesn't look as though we will be able to continue there. It is too hard to fully comprehend really.*

At the end of conference, we shared a meal with Larry and Linda at a restaurant on our way to the airport. They were on our same flight to Ujung Pandang before going on to Jakarta. While we ate, a waitress whisked Esther off to the kitchen to babysit her with other staff as waitresses often did, leaving the rest of us to enjoy our meal. So preoccupied were we with the future and so engrossed in discussion, that we were still talking as we walked out to the waiting taxi. Just then a panicking waitress came running out with Esther in her arms to remind us of a far more pressing issue. "Don't forget your baby!"

Once back in Ujung Pandang we spent a month working with Dave Matti and Susan Shore on the library. Susan was about to head off to the southern Philippines to establish a base there for the continued work in exile. We weren't to know how soon after we would have to follow her.

\*\*\*\*

After some delays for our children's health issues, we finally drove north to Mambi. Ambe Hande, the head of Salu Leäng at the time, was there and happy to travel with us once we had managed to arrange for a horse. A possibility of getting one or two from Aralle arose, but next day their owners decided against it and we were back to square one. Ambe Hande thought we might be able to arrange a couple of porters, but Delwyn felt strongly that we should wait for a horse and went upstairs to pray. Later she wrote:

> *I read the story of Moses crossing the Red Sea and had a real sense that this was God's timing for us to go to Tabulahan and that He would make a way. We just needed to trust Him to work it out when it seemed impossible. I felt a real certainty by the time Esther woke that something would*

*work out and we would have a horse. I came down to look for Robin. He was outside with our host's son, sitting down next to a man with a horse. Apparently, this man had been given some money by his brother to buy some horses and when he saw that we needed one he decided to do it right away. I was in a bit of a blur as I realised that we served the God of the impossible. It certainly wasn't what I was expecting!*

Ambe Hande usually travelled the second day over Pote' Leha, the shorter route, which was too steep for horses. He assured us that we would find porters in the village of Ranteberang and that also suited the new owner of the horse. Mama Semeng was not in Taora at the time, so we would have missed her if we had gone that way in any case. Ranteberang was the animist village from where the shaman 'auntie' who had tended Indo Datu hailed. We overnighted in the house of the village head, along with a group of other travellers. It was a vast windowless place with a wooden platform on which a dozen or so of us slept. There were no pillows, mattresses or even mats available, and our children (at that time aged 11 months to just under eight years old), and thus their parents, were restless through the night.

After the next day's steep climb and steep descent our knees were shaky at best, but we had made good time, reaching Salu Leäng by 4:00 p.m. after a short stop to visit Ambe Sone' and other friends in the village of Peu'. Over the course of the next eight days, we were overwhelmed by the welcome we received from all our friends whom we had not seen for 18 months. I'm sure that our new addition provided a lot of the interest. We were especially pleased to meet up with Mariones, now newly married. She gave us two notebooks that she had used to make a first draft of Genesis 12 to 36 and a few chapters of Exodus. Just before we had left for furlough, Delwyn had handed her a scrap of paper scribbled with these chapter numbers as something she could work on in our absence. Once again, she had shown her keenness and trustworthiness. Ever helpful, she also found two teenage girls, Ode and Sambo, to come and stay with us in Palu.

The other goal for this very brief time in the village was the setting up of a translation committee, formed of representatives from the various congregations who would liaise with their congregants about all aspects of the translation and who would also assist with checking any passages we translated for naturalness of language. We were able to see the beginnings of the committee's formation during this short trip.

Then on Esther's first birthday we headed out again along with Ode and Sambo. Travelling with us was Hans, Mama Semeng's son. He was on his way to Ujung Pandang to take money from Mama Ondong for medicine for her son Daud, who was on a long course of medication. We left Mambi early, planning to call in to Mamasa on the way to Polewali. After an hour along the wet mud road, we hit a sharp stone hiding at the bottom of a deep puddle, on which we burst the right-hand side rear tyre. The slick conditions and the camber on the road were such that each time I tried jacking the side of the car up, it slid off the jack. Part of the problem was that the jack itself was under water. After many vain attempts and a crushed thumb, Delwyn's smart thinking came to the rescue and, once we tied the car to a tree down the opposite bank, it stayed on the jack long enough to get the wheel replaced. It had taken three and a half hours though!

A few minutes later we left the mud behind as we reached the newly sealed part of the road. "Hallelujah, we're okay now," was our collective thought. Next minute there was a grinding sound of metal on asphalt. I pulled up and got out to look.

The left-hand front wheel was missing. A minute's searching found it down the bank 20 metres back. On closer examination I saw that the whole hub had come off, stripping threads in the process. We had nothing to fix this one with. And the fact that it was not our own vehicle added extra pressure. I felt like one of Elisha's companions losing the head of a borrowed axe. More cause for prayer.

Another Land Cruiser came from the opposite direction, one of the regulars for fare-paying passengers. We were blocking the narrow road, so there was no way they could continue. The driver was a resourceful man, armed with a box of miscellaneous parts. Among them he found a used hub that would work if he forced it on with a hammer, cold chisel and brute force. He suggested we stop and check it regularly in case it should come loose again. This we did after 100 metres, 200 metres, 500 metres, five kilometres, ten kilometres. We were on our way once more, albeit without 4WD, as the automatic locking hub was now defunct. In Mamasa we visited Mama Yoni and I foolishly took advice to park the car down a narrow right-angled entrance with a ditch alongside. The tight reverse turn took us into the ditch, and I had to find another 4WD to tow us out again. That evening I took a jeweller's screwdriver and bored a hole in my crushed thumbnail to relieve the pressure and the throbbing. It was that kind of day.

All this time I was keenly aware that I had miscalculated the funds we needed to get us back to Palu. This would mean that we would need to detour to Ujung Pandang and back to Pinrang (an extra six to eight hours driving) to get the Rp. 200,000 we were lacking. When Hans told me that the money he was taking for Daud's medicine was Rp. 200,000, I realised that a phone call from Polewali could save us the extra driving and Hans a trip to Ujung Pandang that he also would not have to make. On arrival at Polewali I rang the office to arrange for

Christine Varley to take money from our account. Christine had once visited Daud with us and knew his address, so I asked if she would take the money and deliver it to Daud for his medicine. That done, Hans gave us Daud's money, and we were then able to continue on our way while Hans returned to the village. While talking with Christine, she intimated that we needed to get back to Palu as soon as possible as she had heard there were problems with our visa, and we would need to get in touch with the Jakarta office without delay.

Continuing to periodically check the wheel, we headed for Palopo, where there was a Tabulahan family with whom we could overnight. It was beginning to get dark as we neared the town when suddenly the steering started to feel strange. I checked the wheel again. It seemed fine. I checked the right-hand wheel. Like its left-hand mate had been, it was on its way to falling off! Fortunately, we were only a few minutes from our destination and so continued at a snail's pace.

Next morning our host told me of a large garage nearby where I should be able to get the wheel problems sorted. Somehow, I missed it completely and ended up at a small enterprise owned by a mechanic who turned out to be one of the keenest followers of Jesus I ever met in Sulawesi. For the next three hours the car was worked on by two of his team while we had a great time of fellowship. The car fixed and my spirit uplifted, I returned to pick up the others and we continued north to Palu, overnighting in Pendolo. Before we had left Salu Leäng, someone had told Ode and Sambo that the key to not getting car sick was to sing. They had been doing so almost constantly for the past two days, going through the hymn book verse by verse from memory! Now as we left Palopo we were all singing.

\*\*\*\*

The news from Jakarta was not good. We were told that our long-term visa was not going to be granted and we would have to leave the country again. This time, we were told, it would not be for a short-term wait, and that Davao in the Philippines was the best option. There was less than a month remaining on our current visa. The next three weeks were busy. First, we broke the news to Ode and Sambo that they would have to return to the village just a week or two after leaving there. Fortunately, there was a distant relative resident in Palu who was able to travel with them. Second, we booked our flights from Palu to Davao via Manado. Third, we got four small crates made to hold the one cubic metre of belongings not being sold or left, then tried to find a way to get them shipped up to Manado and hopefully thence to Davao. At that time information was very difficult to obtain, especially as this was not a well-travelled route and there was no established shipping between these ports. Fourth, we put word around that we were wanting to sell the almost new furniture we had purchased a few months earlier and our old Toyota Land Cruiser, now fixed.

As the weeks passed, the need to sell items, and especially the car, became more of a burden. Delwyn put down her thoughts:

> *I feel in a constant state of grief. The girls we brought will have to return and they are doing so well too. Every now and then I just want to cry when I think of moving again. And to a new country when I don't feel the least bit like doing so, or emotionally ready for it. Spiritually, I feel God is in control, but I know I need to keep looking to Him for the strength to go through this. I rest in the fact that if God is not allowing us to stay at this time, He must have a better plan... Still no takers for the car. It would be an*

*enormous relief to get the car sold soon. It doesn't look as though it will be easy for the person who buys it to get the paperwork up from Ujung Pandang. We need a little miracle. I almost feel excited at the thought that the Lord is going to show His faithfulness again to us in this situation.*

A week later our prayers were answered. Our office worker, Markus, was passing the immigration office when an official called out to him and asked if he knew of anyone wanting to sell a car. The official came round immediately, agreed on a price and the deal was done. There was suddenly a stream of other callers from among the immigration office staff, all keen to pick up bargains. They bought a good deal of the furniture at knock down prices. One immigration official was disappointed that Delwyn would not sell him the Roland keyboard we were taking with us, a precious gift from her mother.

We were unable to make contact with a travel agent in Manado but risked sending our four small crates to his address anyway, figuring that by the time they arrived after a two-day bus trip, we would have overtaken them by plane. As it turned out, they arrived before us, Bouraq Airlines having cancelled our flight to Manado twice. This left the poor travel agent scratching his head as to the origin of these mystery crates. As soon as we arrived in the city, we got in touch with the agent and asked if he could find any way of getting our crates across the sea to Davao. A day or two later he had a solution. One of his staff members was a Filipina whose cousin was part of the crew on a small fishing boat operating between Manado and General Santos. They took their catch to either of these ports and occasionally carried other items. The cousin would then arrange for the crates to travel overland from General Santos to Davao.

At the same time that we lost our visas and were told to go

to Davao, the Matti family in Ujung Pandang were given the same instructions. They arrived in Manado the same day as us and we found a small hotel to accommodate us all. It was wonderful to have friends to share the new experiences. At that time there were two flights a week from Manado to Davao. We were scheduled to leave on the next flight two or three days after our arrival. Then Bouraq Airlines decided to cancel the tickets of the few pre-booked passengers in favour of a later block booking that would fill the plane. This meant another four days in the hot, cramped conditions of the hotel. We asked if Bouraq would pay our extra accommodation costs. They refused.

Next day Delwyn and Sharon took the three older children and the two babies-in-arms into the Bouraq office and asked very politely and quietly (apart from the crying babies) if there was any other compensation we were allowed, such as help with excess baggage, since we were moving to a new country long term. The manager went away to make a phone call, then came back with a sternly delivered message that they would grant us 100 kilos of excess baggage and no more between the nine of us. Any over that would be charged the full excess price. This was great news. At three dollars a kilo, that was more than the cost of an extra four nights in the hotel. The Mattis had quite a bit of excess baggage and we had a little. At the airport on the way out we discovered that the total weighed in at 99 kilos excess. Thank You, Lord!

The plane that was to fly us back and forth for the next few years was a Hawker-Siddeley 748 twin turboprop that had already seen many years of service. The flight took an hour and forty minutes at a height of just 11,000 feet, affording great views of the Sangir Islands between Indonesia and the Philippines, of Mt Apo and of Samal Island in the Davao Gulf as we came in to land. And then we had arrived. Another new country.

## 14

# Davao

A new country is always interesting. If you have had enough time to anticipate the move and make plans, discovering all the new experiences can be exciting. We had had very little time to get used to the idea of being transplanted to a country we had not signed up for. Our focus was firmly on Indonesia. What would living in the Philippines be like? More importantly, would it be possible to continue the translation when separated from its heartland? Would anyone be able and willing to come and work with us in an overseas setting? With questions like these very much on our minds, it took us a few weeks to get used to being in a city that later we came to love.

Susan Shore had been the first of the Sulawesi exodus to arrive and settle in Davao. After a few weeks of staying in the OMF guest house, she had just rented an apartment of her own in a small, gated complex. And here she graciously put up the McKenzie tribe for the next month while we got our bearings and found our own apartment to rent. It was now a week since our crates had been shipped from Manado. Naively, we thought they may even have arrived before us. As the weeks ticked by and phone calls to Manado revealed only mystery as to their whereabouts, we began to despair of ever seeing them again. Then, one day, a month after they were shipped, a jeepney pulled up outside Susan's place and in it was the fisherman cousin and our crates. He explained that the crates would have been destroyed in breaking them open for customs inspection back in General Santos, so he had paid the official something to look the other way. I had wrongly thought customs inspection would be at final delivery point, as it had been for my family's crates on arrival in Christchurch from England. I thanked the fisherman, paid the balance and a little extra for his trouble.

Like our last month in Indonesia, our first two or three months in the Philippines were an emotional strain for all of us, especially Delwyn who was feeling the unsettledness of the children keenly. Most of her journal entries at that time reflect a state of discouragement bordering on depression. Often minor things, like leaving the backpack baby carrier in a taxi, became out-of-proportion strains. Nevertheless, there were lessons in each of these incidents. Delwyn wrote:

> *I have been so upset that I left Esther's backpack on a P.U. (taxi) yesterday. We depend heavily on it for getting around with her. But it has been a reminder of how more upset I get with lost <u>things</u> than with lost people. God, grant me the eyes to see how You view the world and the lost around me.*

After four weeks staying with Susan, we found an affordable, centrally located upstairs apartment directly above our landlord's house. It was spacious enough to accommodate future Tabulahan men, should that happen, and had an office in which we might work on translation. It was, however, the hottest house of the 18 we lived in while overseas. The children had constant heat rash, somewhat soothed by putting them to bed wet from their shower and with a fan blasting them. We lived here for the next two years and three months. It took us a year and a half to finally get around to buying a couple of air conditioners. I guess some people are just slow.

Davao was a world of new experiences. Of course, we had now been living in insular southeast Asia for the past half dozen years, but each country has its uniqueness. The Philippines is its own unique blend of Asianness and Western influence. Heritage from its Spanish colonial past is seen in names of places and people and in words and phrases adopted into the local languages. Heritage from its American colonial past is observable in the widespread use of English, especially in the cities. We were soon to learn that fluency in English among the local population did not mean we would be automatically understood by those we conversed with. We had to learn to use the right words. Our landlord could not understand us when we asked where we should put out the 'rubbish'. We tried 'trash'. Still no joy. Finally, 'garbage' was understood, and we found there was a daily collection out on the street at the end of our alley.

I was approached by a young woman in a church who asked, "May I solicit you?" I was a little confused, but eventually worked out that she was asking for sponsorship to attend a Christian young professionals conference. Some expat friends later pointed out to us that 'solicitor' can mean salesperson, rather than lawyer or something else.

We also found that we needed to develop a post-vocalic 'r' to be understood. Our American colleagues used the r-sound no matter where it appeared within a syllable, whereas most Kiwis tend to use it with a clear sound only at the start of a syllable. Though our colleagues had almost always understood our dialect, our new neighbours in the Philippines needed us to supply an 'r' wherever it would be written. An early example of this was when Delwyn went to a convenience store down the street to see if she could buy some butter.

"Do you sell butta?" she asked the attendant.

"No, Ma'am."

"Really? I would have thought you would sell butta."

"No, Ma'am. We don't have that one."

Delwyn wandered the store for a minute and found a tub of margarine. She took this back to the counter. "Butta is like margarine."

"Oh, mar-ga-ri-na. Yes, we have margarina."

"Well, butta is like margarina."

"Sorry, Ma'am, out of stock.

Delwyn had another wander around the store and finally found butter in a cooler. She picked up a block and brought it to the counter.

"Oh yes, Ma'am, we have Anchorrr butterrr." And that is how we pronounced it thereafter.

We soon had our apartment set up with mattresses on the floor, bamboo furniture in the living room and a couple of tables tacked together for writing desks. We also purchased a fridge, a small washing machine and fans to circulate the ever-hot air. Using a crate for a desk, Delwyn resumed correspondence school lessons for Fraser, with two pre-schoolers busily trying to enrol. There was an international school nearby: Faith Academy, Davao (FAD), which provided elementary and middle schooling for the children of missionaries and other expatriates working in Davao. High schoolers generally went to board in Manila. After a few months we decided to enrol Fraser at FAD. Delwyn taught Isaac with correspondence school lessons initially before he too joined his brother. Esther was to follow this pattern too when she started school.

Meanwhile, I had to head back to Indonesia to close the Palu office, while Dave Matti went to do the same in Ujung Pandang. We had not done so before we left, because the situation was still unclear at that point. Now that it was certain there would be no continued official presence in those cities, we were to return, package up the libraries and essential files for shipment to Davao, burn non-essential files, sell group assets, like office furniture and vehicles, and return rented properties to their respective landlords. It was an opportunity also for me to make a quick trip to Tabulahan in the hope of finding a couple of young men free from commitments and willing to come and stay with us in the Philippines. This was a big ask, but something we prayed for despite our doubts. It had been difficult enough to find young men to work with us in the village. We had also drawn blanks trying to get young men to work with us in Palu. Now I needed to find some who were willing to work overseas. As far as I was aware, only one Tabulahan man had ever left the country.

A song that was a great encouragement to us at this time of uncertainty, and perhaps the theme song of much of our overseas journey, was Don Moen's: 'God will make a way when there seems to be no way' (and its Indonesian equivalent, '*Tuhan buka jalan saat tak ada jalan*'). We often sang this with friends and colleagues while we were still in Indonesia. And here again, we were singing it in the Philippines with the Mattis and others. Delwyn prayed that the Lord would not only open the way but give me a peace in my heart about the right men when I found them.

Passing through Ujung Pandang on my way to Palu, I made some enquiries among the local Tabulahan community. One older man said his nephew would come with me. I had not yet met the nephew and so had my doubts, but his uncle assured me that he would do as he was told and go. I did meet another young man who was willing, although something about him gave me reservations. Anyway, on the strength of this brief contact, and knowing that she would understand that there would be two Tabulahan men coming, I sent a message to Delwyn through Dave Matti, who was ringing his wife in Davao. Sharon and Delwyn were taking the children to the beach the next day when Sharon passed on the message. "Dave said that Robin said to tell you to order two beds." Apparently Delwyn 'cried and cried with tears of joy' at the answer to prayer. As it happened, the prayer was not answered the way I was thinking, as neither of these young men worked out, but the Lord knew that Delwyn needed that encouragement to type up all that Mariones had drafted. And, besides, He had already sorted out the ones to come.

It was the first time I had been to the village without Delwyn and the children since my first trip. Even then I was one of a party of three. It felt so different taking public transport to Mambi. And, although I had done this walk alone a few times, I felt unusually lonely on the two-day hike from there. This time my family would not be there when I reached the village. I found a new respect for the unmarried translators who worked alone in their language groups, courageous women like Donna Evans and, later, Susan Shore.

I could only spend a few days in the village area in which to find suitable young men before heading to Palu to close down the office. I met with translation committee members and explained that we could no longer remain long term in Indonesia but could continue the project offshore if we had people to work with, preferably young men without too many other commitments. One or two suggestions were made, but each had a reason for not being suitable or available. The time was running out. I would soon have to leave the village to go to Palu and I still had no one lined up. As usual I was staying with the minister and his household. When he heard that I still had not found someone, Pa' Pandita suggested his grandson, Daud. Mama Ondong concurred that her son would be a good choice. I knew Daud to be a capable young man who had been studying for a degree in agriculture in Ujung Pandang. But I also knew he had stopped studying because of prolonged illness. Now, his mother and grandfather assured me that he was fit and well again. He had been on a long course of medication and was now free of the disease. And they were both happy for him to go overseas.

"What about his studies?" I asked.

"Oh, he took a year out because of his illness. So basically, he is doing nothing at the moment."

"Is he still living in Ujung Pandang?"

"No, he is staying with his uncle in Polewali. I am sure he would love to work with you in the Philippines. But you would need to ask him when you pass through Polewali."

"Yes, I certainly will. Can you think of anyone else suitable who might want to come too?"

"What about Ando', Daud's cousin."

I knew Ando' as well. He was another young man I thought would be excellent to work with at some time in the future—perhaps once he had finished his theological studies. "Isn't he studying theology?" I asked.

"Yes, he was. But he dropped out due to lack of funds."

"Where is he now?"

"He is back here in the village. You should go down to Sohongang and ask him and his father if he can go."

If this worked out, I would leave the village first thing in the morning. It was getting dark as I headed down to Sohongang. Papa Emang greeted me at the kitchen door and invited me to join the family for the evening meal. He was pleased to be able to offer something special to go along with the rice and leaves—sago grubs. It was the first and last time I ever tried them. In short, not my favourite fare. However, it was a good meeting and Papa Emang was certain Ando' would want to go to work with us in the Philippines. When Ando' showed up after dark I asked him and explained that I hoped Daud would want to come too. He was keen and said he would go down to Polewali in two- or three-days' time and travel with Daud to Ujung Pandang to get their passport process started. I was elated. The Lord had organised the two young men, whom I had already thought would be good to work with, to be available at the time we needed them.

Two days later I stepped down from the van at the Polewali bus station, booked myself on the next bus to Ujung Pandang and caught a bicycle rickshaw round to Papa Abri's house. Daud was not there. Papa and Mama Abri were uncertain as to when he might return, but definitely by evening. The problem was that my bus was to leave within the hour. I explained to them my reason for wanting to see him and wrote a letter for them to pass on to him. Then I thanked them and headed back to the bus station. Just before I boarded the bus, I spotted Daud walking past the station. I hailed him and hurriedly explained my hopes and his mother's and grandfather's permission and that Ando' would be coming too. He was keen to come and agreed to meet me in Ujung Pandang in a week's time. "Further details are in the letter left with Papa Abri," I explained.

I left money for their passports and tickets at the Ujung Pandang office, along with details about what the two of them would need to do to get their passports. Hopefully that process would be well underway by the time I got back from Palu in a week or so.

Next day I caught a flight there and set about boxing up library books and sorting through office files—which ones to take, which to burn—and thinking about how best to sell unwanted office furniture and other assets. Two or three of my colleagues were also back in town sorting out their own house lots on behalf of their families left in America. It made sense for us all to stay in one house and share the evening meal before we went our separate ways each morning. It was a good time of fellowship each evening after a long day of sorting.

*Davao*

Once back in Ujung Pandang, I met up with Daud and Ando' who were now waiting for their passports to be issued. This would likely take another week. I was scheduled to be returning to the Philippines in the next couple of days. I also met up with Phil and Denise Campbell, who, like the others I had seen in Palu, were sorting their belongings with a view to heading to the Philippines. Phil and Denise kindly agreed to have Daud and Ando' travel with them, as it was to be the first time travelling internationally for the young men—indeed, their first time flying.

What a pleasure it was, a week later, to welcome not just the Campbells, but the two young men who were the answers to many prayers. It was the beginning of a new chapter in the translation of the Tabulahan Scriptures. For the first time I had regular co-workers. For the first time there would be no interruptions for weddings and funerals and trail work parties and coffee picking and rice processing. It felt as if the Lord had opened a door wide in response to the closed window.

## 15

# Translation

Daud and Ando' were among the more educated of Tabulahan speakers. Still, they were unaccustomed to writing in their own language and had as yet no understanding of translation principles. So, for the first couple of weeks of working together, we spent most of our time practising writing in various genres and editing texts that had been adulterated with deliberate grammatical errors, or with 'bad style', then in lessons in translation principles, with exercises in translating material from Indonesian to Tabulahan. They were both quick learners and we soon moved on to revising the portions of Genesis already drafted, and then completing the remaining 11 chapters. Mariones had also worked with me on the miracle passages from Mark's Gospel, so we took these as a starting point in drafting the remainder of Mark.

By mid-April we had a first draft of both these books. This did not mean that Genesis and Mark were almost ready for publication. The first draft is just that—a first draft. Each portion needs to be run through several checks, with different participants for each of these.

Of course, not all of these participants in the process would be able to be brought to the Philippines. Our plan was to draft portions and check for accuracy in Davao, then periodically return to Tabulahan for comprehension and naturalness checks. Final checks with consultants could be made wherever

> ### Accuracy, Clarity, Naturalness:
> ### The Checking Process
>
> The first draft is checked against a literal translation for accuracy, ensuring that nothing is left out and nothing is added (apart from implied information that the original hearers would have understood that the modern hearers may need to have explained).
>
> The translation also needs to be clear, so it is checked for comprehension with several mother-tongue speakers not involved in its translation, using questions appropriate for the passage.
>
> A committee of reviewers then checks through the translation for anything that may sound unnatural in their language. Adjustments are made from each of these kinds of checks.
>
> Finally, a consultant goes through each passage with the translators and at least one mother-tongue speaker who has not worked on the book, asking questions based on a back-translation (i.e., a literal rendering from the target language back into English or another language the consultant understands). The consultant is aiming to pick up any loose ends: errors in initial exegesis, overall readability and comprehension by a new reader or hearer of the passages. After this long process the end product should be Scripture that communicates accurately God's message in a clear and natural way.

we could get all necessary participants together, either in the Philippines or Indonesia. The first of these was a check of Mark's Gospel and some of Genesis which took place in

Mamasa with consultant Marge Crofts. Marge was in the area for consultant checks on other languages too, so we were able to coincide with that timing immediately after our first village trip from the Philippines as a family.

The time in the village had gone well. I was able to spend time with the newly established translation committee giving them input on translation principles and the kinds of things to be looking out for in the material. They each received copies of what had been translated to review for naturalness. Much of the rest of our time had been taken up with checking Mark's Gospel and Genesis for comprehension with a few other folk.

Meanwhile, the children were readjusting to village life with all its adventures. This was a lot more educational than the little bit of home-schooling that was going on for Fraser and Isaac. Since returning from furlough, we always stayed upstairs with our host family. Our little flatette on the ground had been dismantled and our remaining household items distributed. One of the family highlights each day happened straight after the evening meal. With no light other than that provided by small kerosene wicks, everyone went to bed soon after dinner. The lack of light made it difficult to even read bed-time stories to the children. So, in the months leading up to a village trip I would jot down all the jokes I came across and would dole some of these out each night. For variety, we sometimes told each other mystery scenarios to work out: things like, "Each day a man goes down in the elevator on his way to work, then after work walks up the stairs to his apartment. Why?" And occasionally we played a game like the BBC radio program, *Just a Minute*.

Esther turned two during this trip and was daily adding to her vocabulary. For the coming years, birthdays became a minor feature of our annual pilgrimage to the village. To fit in with school holidays, we planned to spend June and July in Indonesia. This encompassed Esther's, Fraser's and my birthdays. On this particular trip Fraser's birthday coincided with the day we were hiking to Taora on our way out to Mamasa for the consultant check. We knew Mama Semeng would not be in Taora, as she was in Tabulahan at the time, but she had told us to use her house as we passed through. Delwyn was not feeling great when we arrived in Taora mid-afternoon and needed to take some paracetamol and lie down for a while. I chatted with the men travelling with us and watched the children. Late in the afternoon I woke Delwyn and reminded her that as the only adult female in the party it was culturally expected that she would cook the evening meal. She was still not feeling great but was glad of the rest and got up to light the fire while I went off to buy some noodles and tinned sardines.

We were both feeling that it would not be much of a ninth birthday party for our son. As a gift for him we had brought a small GI Joe soldier with a little rubber dinghy that we had bought at a garage sale. It was only a small gift, but it was the meal we felt was really lacking. Delwyn cooked up the rice we had brought with us and the fish and noodles I had just bought at a small kiosk—enough for us all, including the men travelling with us. We were just sitting down to give thanks before eating when a voice called from outside the door. A couple of Taora folk were standing there holding two bowls of food. "Tomorrow we are holding the annual wedding," one of them said. "Nine couples will be married, so we have been cooking all day. We thought you might like some of the meat and vegetables." We thanked them profusely and brought the bowls to the table. Under the lid of one were some greens cooked village style. Under the lid of the other was the most delicious pork we had ever had in the area, cooked in sweet soy sauce, no less!

"Look what the Lord has provided for your birthday," Delwyn said to Fraser. We then resumed giving thanks and praying a blessing on the birthday boy. Fraser began to cry.

"What's the matter?" we asked.

"I'm just so glad I have such good parents." And we all got a bit misty.

Once in Mamasa we located Mama Yoni as a Tabulahan speaker not involved in the translation. Ando' and Daud had travelled with us to give their input as co-translators. And we met up with Marge as consultant. Marge worked internationally, consulting on translations in many countries since completing her own New Testament translation in Brazil. She especially liked helping new translators get off to a good start—very encouraging at what had been done well, while pulling no punches when some issue needed addressing. She was the same age as Mama Yoni and immediately established a good rapport with her.

The first days I found quite tiring. I was used to working with Daud and Ando' using Tabulahan as a medium of communication. And when doing comprehension checks with other speakers, we were again using just that one language. Now, for the consultant check, I was suddenly having to translate all Marge's exegetical questions for Daud or Ando', or comprehension questions for Mama Yoni, and then translate their answers into English for Marge. I confess there were times in the afternoons when I ended up using the wrong language for the listener's ear!

While we were looking at the passage where Jesus was anointed at Bethany (Mark 14:1-9), Marge asked Mama Yoni why she thought the woman had poured out such expensive perfume on Jesus. Mama Yoni didn't answer straight away. Then after a pause she said, "She didn't care that it was expensive. She just wanted to show how much she loved Jesus."

Marge began to cry. And for the next few minutes we had to stop while she wept, at the end of which she said, "You know, I have consulted on this book more than a hundred times and every time I have been touched at some point by the power of the gospel."

After finishing the check of Mark there were still some days available, so we ploughed into Genesis. Mama Yoni was not available for some of this, but a young man named Sone' was able to fill in. At this point we had worked through all the other checks, but I had not yet completed the backtranslation. So, each evening, after checking all day, I worked on the backtranslation for Marge. We were not able to complete Genesis in the time available but got over halfway. It was an exhausting but very fulfilling time.

Daud wished to continue his studies following the consultant check, rather than return to Davao. We asked Sone' if he would like to come in his place. Ambe Sone', his father, was the translation committee member for the village of Peu'. He had already asked me if his son could join us in the Philippines at some point in the future. Sone' was keen, so that was settled. It would be November before they would follow us to the Philippines. By then I would have done some preparatory work for future translation and lined up a consultant check of the remainder of Genesis. Ando' was now a seasoned traveller and able to help Sone' through the travel document process.

Once back in the Philippines school activities resumed for the boys. And outside of school there was piano. Isaac had earlier been intrigued by watching his mother at the piano and had decided he wanted to learn. He was almost five at that point. Fraser then decided to get in on the act and started lessons soon after. A few of their friends followed and the Suzuki piano class was born. Esther was too young for piano at this stage but was getting into singing. Music became more and more a part of all our lives as Delwyn was co-opted to teach some music classes at FAD. She was asked to put on something for Christmas and worked on songs for a short musical. This meant I was also co-opted to help with script, lyrics and staging. It was a creative outlet in the evenings.

During a debriefing at the office, our director pointed out that we had not gone anywhere for a vacation in the past two years since furlough. We said that we had not done so during the last four-year field term either—there was more than enough travel in our lives. We had been content with day trips now and then to a local beach. He said we all needed a complete break once in a while and should plan to go somewhere for a week. The last thing we wanted to do was go overseas again, but we had heard that the Philippine branch of SIL had a base in Mindanao that was a very restful spot. This was Nasuli, where most of the teams working on the languages of the southern Philippines were at home when not out in the villages.

Kiwi friends, the Hunts, worked in the Matigsalug language and offered us the use of their home in Nasuli for a week during one of their times of staying in the village. It was a slice of heaven once there and an interesting experience getting there. After a dusty six-hour bus trip, we boarded a crowded jeepney for the last few kilometres. Though seemingly impossible, there were more passengers on the roof than inside. And the conductor took fares through the windows while clinging to the outsides as we whizzed along the road at 100 kilometres per hour!

Nasuli was a delightful place: a collection of individually owned wooden houses in a park-like setting scattered around group housing, offices, caretakers' sheds, a library and a meeting hall. At one end a hangar separated a grass airstrip from the rest of the centre. And the jewel in the setting was the spring-fed pool surrounded by tall, buttressed trees. Although Nasuli was a hive of activity for all who lived there, it was the most restful of places for a visitor. We enjoyed long walks on the airstrip where the uninterrupted views over the fields and up into the expanse above made a huge bowl of the sky. We enjoyed book reading in the relative cool of the house or in the shade of the huge trees. And at least once a day we enjoyed a swim in the clear waters of the spring. We returned to Davao after a week well rested and with no doubts as to where we would go for our next vacation.

It was following this holiday week in Nasuli that we bought two air conditioners. The coolness of the air at about 2,000 feet was so refreshing and such a contrast to the heat and humidity of the coast. Arriving back in Davao to our sweltering apartment, we realised we had to do something about it and had the air conditioning units installed a day or two later. What a difference they made to both well-being and productivity. The children's heat rash reduced immediately, everyone was happier and, with my back no longer dripping with sweat, I could sit at the computer for longer periods without taking a shower.

When Ando' returned in November, with Sone' as Daud's replacement, we were able to make good strides in drafting some more passages of the Word. After getting Sone' jump-started with a short course in translation principles and beginning work with Ando' on Acts, we revised and completed a first draft of Exodus 1 to 20 during December. Then in January we had the last 19 chapters of Genesis checked with consultant Bob Sterner who was now living in Davao. Sone' was again able to help in completing this check in the role he had had for the first 31 chapters. This meant we would be able to prepare Genesis as well as Mark for publication as Scripture portions for distribution.

From late January to late February, I worked with Sone' on some narrative passages from John's Gospel, and with Ando', continuing a computer-assisted adaptation of Acts from the neighbouring Bambam language. Then in March and April we all worked together to complete a first draft of I & II Timothy and Titus. When not working with me on Scripture translation—that is, during the times when I was working with the other—Sone' and Ando' worked on other projects, such as translating hymns, writing a vernacular recipe book, entering texts into the computer and adding to the ongoing project of the Tabulahan–Indonesian–English dictionary.

Twice a week there were classes held for any Indonesian co-translators currently in Davao. These were taught by SIL staff on a rotational basis. The Wednesday afternoon class was on aspects of linguistics and translation and was held in Indonesian. On Monday afternoons there was an English conversation class. Learning some English helped the men in getting around the city in their free time and in conversing with others who could not speak Indonesian. When any of our co-translators were out and about, local folk would assume they were Filipinos and speak to them in Cebuano or Tagalog. A few words of broken English soon corrected the mistake. Some Cebuano words sounded like Tabulahan words but had quite different meanings. On more than one occasion our co-translators have been on a jeepney when the driver has wanted everyone to pack in tighter to allow for another passenger to board. "Urung! Urung!" he would say. This invariably led to smirks from the Tabulahan men. To a Tabulahan speaker *urung* means 'kiss'!

It was not all work and study, though. Twice a week in the late afternoon there were social sports events held at FAD. These were family get togethers as well as a physical outlet for the desk-bound. Basketball is huge in the Philippines, with competitive leagues and even many games played on narrow streets. In Indonesia it ranks far lower down the popular sports scale, so the Indonesian men always gravitated to the game of soccer being held on the field. They also took part in the annual school track and field day, with the one-kilometre and three-kilometre runs being open to all. And of course, there were excursions with the family to a place of interest, such as the eagle sanctuary at Malagos, the crocodile farm at Talomo, or one of the local beaches.

In late April Ando' and Sone' returned to Tabulahan. A month later our family followed them, after a stop off in Manado to attend the Indonesia branch conference at which I was a delegate. After deducting conference and travel time from our two-month visa, this would cut down village time to just five weeks, in which we hoped to check all that we had been working on in the preceding months. On the previous trip to the village, we had reported in Mambi as usual. And the district head had said to me, "We know you. You don't need to report here each time. You can go direct to the village through Mamuju if you like." So, from then on, we did. This would cut off a day's walk in each direction.

Ando' met us in Ujung Pandang and travelled with us from there. This would be the first time we were to use the northerly route since drowning our car crossing the Kalukku River six years earlier. This time, however, we had no car and so took the night bus along the coast to Mamuju, arriving at 7:00 a.m. on Esther's third birthday. From there we took a minivan to Le'beng and then a 4WD inland to Lakähäng. Ando' and I were on the roof with a few other men; the boys were squashed in the back; Delwyn, trying to keep her feet from burning on the exhaust pipe below them while holding Esther, was seated between the driver and a lady who was carrying three trays of eggs. At one point the egg lady produced a half-melted ice-block and gave it to Esther—another unexpected birthday treat! Then at Kumaka our scattered family let out a collective "Wow!" as we came down the hill to the newly erected bridge spanning the river of such strong memories.

The next day as we walked in through the mud, I slipped while carrying Esther and landed heavily against her knee. She seemed none the worse for it, but I may have cracked a rib or two. The following days the pain grew worse and worse and gradually eased over the next weeks. Once we were in the village area, Delwyn helped me out in carrying Esther when we went visiting, and Fraser carried his sister when neither of us could. Although it was a truncated village visit, we were able to accomplish all our goals. At the end of that time, we travelled through Mamasa to seek the church synod's seal of approval for Scripture portions, which would mean Mark, Genesis and future portions could be published locally in Sulawesi, rather than in Java after a lengthy time-lag. (Some colleagues had waited three years to get Mark published under other auspices.) The meeting with the synod leadership went well. They agreed to have the books and future portions published in their name.

Sone' had been in Mamasa until the last week of our time in the village, when he arrived for his sister's wedding. He confided that his employer in Mamasa wanted him to carry on working there, rather than having time off again to return to Davao. We mentioned the situation to Mariones and she suggested we take her youngest brother, Äto'. He had been away at school, so we had not got to know him yet, but we trusted her assessment of him as someone very capable. As had been the case with Sone', a plus with taking Äto' as a new future co-translator to Davao was that he could assist in the next consultant checks of material he had not had any part in. There would be opportunity in the coming months to check the first 20 chapters of Exodus, I & II Timothy and Titus with one consultant and then Acts with another. In between, we planned to spend some time on other literature projects to foster vernacular literacy.

The first of these was working together with Ando' and Äto' at a 'shell book' workshop. The shell book concept could quickly produce bilingual books for any number of local languages. Pre-formatted files containing Indonesian text and line-drawn illustrations needed only the vernacular translations to be inserted and checked, before being ready for publication. Topics of these simple readers ranged from folk tales to agricultural helps, and health advice to Bible stories.

The second workshop was all about investigating local folktales with a view to better understanding the belief systems of the people groups whose languages we were working on. We had already accumulated quite a collection of folktales from the writing competition. Now we had time and impetus to find the best of them, discover commonalities among them and think about implications for translating biblical concepts in a meaningful way. We were also able to select the best of them for a volume of folk tales as another aid to helping Tabulahan people get into reading their own language.

This had been a shorter field term than our first—just three years—but it had been very eventful. When Ando' and Äto' left in November we were looking forward to heading back to New Zealand for our second period of home assignment.

## 16

# Grieving

The results of a survey I once read showed that the thing expatriate New Zealanders miss most while away from home is spending time in solitary places—so much of the world is crowded. Once again as we left the airport for the drive through our home city we wondered where everyone was. Was it a public holiday? No, this was just a normal day in Christchurch. And so, the reverse culture shock adjustments began again. At least this time we had arrived in summer, and so avoided *thermal* shock.

It was again a wonderful time of meeting up with family and friends, with individuals and groups that had been supporting us in various ways, and of making a few new friends. Again, we shared at our home fellowship and at several other venues. Our theme song for this time back home was an invitation to join us in various aspects of prayer for the Bibleless people groups.\*

A highlight for all of us was drinking in New Zealand's fresh air in some out of the way places. This included a trip with a special Australian visitor. Christine Varley, who had visited us in Tabulahan that first Christmas there, joined us for a camping holiday touring the South Island from Arthurs Pass down the west coast, through central Otago to Fiordland and back through the Mackenzie Country. We met up with my

---

\* See song: 'Come With Us'

brother and his family near Queenstown and travelled with them from that point. The cousins enjoyed getting to know each other better, and it was also exciting to hunt some wild food in the shape of fish and rabbits.

For all the highlights, our stay in New Zealand had its tough times. Midway through furlough Delwyn became unexpectedly pregnant. This was a surprise for both of us and difficult for Delwyn who experienced all day nausea. Because of past problems we decided to stay in New Zealand until after the baby was born and maybe bring a co-translator to work with us there. After a few weeks we were getting used to the idea of child number four and beginning to feel positive about it all. Then a scan after ten weeks revealed that the baby had died two weeks earlier, necessitating a D&C. This was an even bigger shock and emotionally quite draining. The experience left us feeling, "What was all that about?" Perhaps it would help us better identify with the many Tabulahan folk who had lost children in one way or another. Delwyn found comfort in the opening verses of Hosea 6.

> *Come, let us return to the Lord. He has torn us to pieces but he will heal us; he has injured us but he will bind up our wounds. (Hosea 6:1)*

Though she felt 'torn to pieces', there was the promise of the Lord's healing, bandaging of wounds and restoration, and also the appropriate response in verse 3: "*Let us press on to acknowledge him.*"

On returning to Davao, we spent the next few months renting the homes of furloughing colleagues, rather than immediately looking for somewhere of our own to rent. For me, it was good to be back and to have Ando' and Äto' back with us continuing the work, but there are always adjustments in new situations. One of the houses we occupied was on a busy street with noise and dust filtering incessantly through the mosquito netting that covered the windows. As Christmas approached, there was the increased stress of church activities and shops and streets getting busier than ever. At the same time Delwyn was struggling with all the adjustments.

> *Sunday, 22 December 96. Not an easy day. Church was just constant noise with people chatting at the back all the time. Lunch was hideous. Everyone just pushed in with little thought for those at the back of the queue. Esther was intolerable (probably because of the chaos) and I came home angry and even more fed up than yesterday. I hate living here. I'm sick of the noise, the dust, the food, the water, the heat (and this is the cool time of the year). I hate myself for being so selfish and feel like I'm in a downward spiral. God help me. To top it all off, it hit me today that I was supposed to be having a baby in the next couple of weeks. I would have still been in New Zealand.*

She knew the way out of the spiral, though. That same day's journal entry continues with a 17-bullet point *'Thank You List for the Lord'*. Despite ongoing issues that sapped her energy, like trying to balance the extended household's needs and fretting over the children's health, the Lord gave her encouragements. One day in early January, she told me how she wished she had brought certain pieces of written music from New Zealand, particularly Gershwin's 'An American in Paris'. That morning she went out to try to find some piano music suitable for some beginners, children of colleagues. And in a poky little shop that sold all sorts of things like reading glasses, there was also some sheet music: not much for beginners, but some of it more advanced old works, mostly bad photocopies. And there in the middle of it all was 'An American in Paris'! The 'Kiwi in Davao' later wrote: *"It was as though God wanted to tell me in a special way that He loved me."*

Early in the year Ando', Äto' and I worked on revising passages from I & II Samuel and I Kings that Ando' had drafted and translating 15 psalms to be published all together as *Life of King David*. We had also begun work on Revelation, which Äto' and Ando' continued to draft together while I was taking part in a discourse analysis workshop. I was able to give them some input in the evenings, and Delwyn was around during the day if they had any queries, but, as its picture language is similar to descriptive/narrative passages, I thought they would be able to work through a lot of it without too much difficulty. At some point they had a disagreement which developed into a complete falling out. Delwyn and I tried to broker a peace agreement between them, praying for them and with them, but nothing seemed to help. After a few days of not speaking to one another, Ando' headed back to Indonesia, leaving Äto' to continue working with us. We remained good friends with Ando' over the years, though he never worked with us on the translation again. We never did find out what the issue was, and it was several years before the two of them reconciled.

Meanwhile Äto' was a fast learner, not only in all that related to translation, but in other things too. He wanted to learn to type properly and did so (something I have never mastered and remain the only one of the family who still uses the two-finger method). He was keen to learn to play the piano and made great strides with the help of Delwyn and the boys. And in his downtime he joined in family sports events, even those he had no experience of, like basketball and even cricket. Delwyn put the recently translated Psalm 23 to music and Äto' quickly learned it on guitar to take back to the village when his visa expired at the end of March.

*Grieving*

Two days after Äto' left, I got the shock of my life. In the early hours of the morning I awoke to find that Delwyn was not in bed with me. Normally when this happened I would assume she was seeing to one of the children and roll over to continue sleeping. For some reason I felt uneasy and got up to find out where she was. I first checked the bathroom. Although the door was unlocked, something was preventing me from opening it. I pushed harder until there was a gap big enough to squeeze through. The hindrance was Delwyn lying up against the door, her head in a pool of blood. My first thought was that someone had broken in and murdered my wife! I checked her pulse—it was still beating, but she was not breathing. I needed to clear her air passage. Her jaws were clamped shut. It took me all my strength to force my fingers behind her molars and forward to pull her jaws apart. Her tongue was back down her throat. It was no easy thing to pull it out. Once I had, there was a sudden inrush of air. Still she was unconscious. Still I didn't know where all the blood had come from. I shook her repeatedly, telling her to say something. Eventually she came around and said she felt awful. I was just so relieved that she felt anything at all!

I cleaned her up and helped her back to bed. It seems she had stomach cramps and must have passed out in the bathroom, fallen hard on the concrete, breaking her nose in the process, whence came the bleeding. The blow on the head must have also triggered a seizure in which she 'swallowed her tongue' and locked her jaws. She stayed in bed all the next day with nausea and vomiting and aching head, neck and limbs. She asked for a mirror. I brought one. One black eye and another on the way, slightly bent and swollen nose, a couple of minor cuts. My eyes were more accurate than the mirror, though—she was still my living, breathing, beautiful wife. Four-year-old Esther was a sweetie. She found a dress she thought would be good to be a nurse in and gave her Mum her favourite teddy bear to cuddle.

Over the succeeding weeks Delwyn began a slow recuperation. Her broken nose and black eyes improved, but her wrist and neck continued to give her pain. As the time approached for returning to Indonesia for our trip to the village area, she began to wonder if she would be able to make it this time. We asked friends to come over and pray with us for her recovery and for peace for the forthcoming trip. Following that, there was a marked improvement in Delwyn's neck pain and more importantly for her inner wellbeing, confident that the Lord would carry us all through.

Just over a week later we were in Manado en route to the village. Delwyn still felt some pain in her wrist, but her neck was much better. She wrote:

*I've had the most incredible peace and deep sense of freedom from fear, and I truly realise I've been carried on the wings of prayer. I just wrote a song: 'When You Pray'. It began with a germ of an idea from an email I wrote to Spreydon [our home church], and I've been mulling it over all day. Can't wait to try it on a piano.*

That would have to be in two months' time, when Delwyn wrote it up back in Davao,* along with the following in a prayer letter home:

### So, who is on the Front Line?

*In a physical battle it is clear who the front-line soldiers are. In the spiritual battle it is perhaps not so clear. Some*

---

\* See song: 'When You Pray'

*think that all who cross the seas to work in a third-world country are going to the front line. But time spent recently in our language area gave me new insight as to what the real 'front line' is.*

*Why was it that from the time we left Davao I felt an overwhelming sense of peace? Why was my neck not troubling me as it had? Why were our travels unusually smooth? Why did I not get frustrated at things that normally would have tested my stress level? Why was it that despite unexpected disappointments I still felt God was in control and he would work out his purposes? Why did we accomplish our goals and even more than we set out to do?*

*It was because of you who prayed – the 'front-liners'. You had already gone to battle on your knees ahead of us. I have no doubt that the reason why so many things fell into place for us is because the battle had already been fought by prayer. We just came in behind those on the front line, shielded by prayer.*

*I want to thank you for being faithful and standing with us in prayer. It means more than you know to have a sense that, although we were isolated, we were not alone.*

Meanwhile, we flew to Ujung Pandang, stayed a day or two in a cheap hotel near the waterfront in order to buy supplies, and then caught the night bus to Mamuju. Meals near the hotel were interesting—delicious, as most Indonesian food is—but with some novelties. We mostly dined at any of a line of mobile carts, on cockroach-ridden benches under a tarpaulin, with plates and cutlery washed in a bucket. I remember asking one vendor what the unusually shaped, chewy meat pieces in my fried rice were. "Chicken," he replied.

"What part of the chicken?" I asked.

He scrounged around for the right piece of Indonesian vocabulary and finally came up with "Its mouth."

I was a little mystified. "Oh, you mean its beak?"

"Yes, that's it. Its beak."

Mystery solved, I finished off the rest of the plate including the dozen little chicken mouths—delish!

After the night bus and a van trip, we spent a few hours visiting Tabulahan folk in Le'beng and caught a crowded 4WD to Lakähäng. It was Esther's fifth birthday—twenty years ago today as I write this. This time there was no ice-block to break the journey for her, but we all got to stretch our legs when one of the wheels fell off. What a contrast to the last time this had happened. I was not the driver and therefore not the one responsible for the repair, nor for the passengers' welfare. I felt quite relieved and confident that it would be quickly sorted, and we would be on our way. Within an hour it was, and we were. As it was a Saturday, we decided to spend Sunday in Lakähäng in order to attend one of the church services there and visit several Tabulahan families in the afternoon. Next day we put Esther and our bags on a horse and hiked into the village area. We arrived in Salu Leäng late afternoon, grateful after a hot, dry walk with all of the children doing really well and Delwyn not in any significant pain.

On arrival we were met with the news that our host, the minister, was not at all well. He had had a stroke that morning and more than one lesser seizure since then. He recognised us and seemed pleased to see us although he was unable to say anything. That night Delwyn dreamed that we were sitting chatting with him. The next morning, he seemed to be doing a little better. He was able to eat and drink a little, sit up, smile and even say a few words. We spent much of the day sitting on the mat with him and other family members who took turns to sit behind him and be the missing armchair to support him.

That evening he began having seizures again. By next morning these were coming at five-minute intervals. This was the day that his daughter, Mama Ondong, had arranged for 20 workers to harvest rice in the big field behind the house. They came—the harvest could not be put off—but it seemed to us an extra pressure that she could do without. She was also concerned that her daughter, Mita, might not get there before her grandfather passed away. Delwyn wrote in her journal entry that day:

> *Mita has just arrived as I'm writing this. I haven't greeted her yet to give her time with the family. Pua' has slept most of the day. Earlier this morning in between seizures he had asked for people to sing and no one was game, so Robin and I sang a few songs before I headed out to do some rice harvesting. It is a day that should be happy—when the harvest is coming in—but it is mingled with sadness as Pua' is so sick. I really feel for Mama Ondong—so many people in the house to feed, workers to see to and her father so unwell.*

The many visitors over those days provided us with ample opportunity to interact with friends and new acquaintances. We were able to talk with people about how they were finding the recently published Scripture portions, namely Mark and Genesis. All who had bought a copy or read someone else's were positive about it and said they could read it fine, even though reading in their own language was still a novelty. The downside of the many visitors was that almost all of the men smoked, and that far into the night. Our two rooms had short walls and no ceiling, so the smoke curled thickly into our rooms as we tried to sleep. Between coughing and going outside for a breather we didn't get a lot of it. It seems mosquito nets are less than adequate as air filters.

A new 'bathroom' had been constructed on the far side of the big rice field. This consisted of three short walls of recycled sago leaf roofing material around a bamboo pipe draining a higher rice terrace. As this pipe was higher than the one in the old 'bathroom' you could get a shower without having to squat, though if you were over four feet tall you would still have to crouch to some extent. It was beside a much-used pathway and the ideal spot for any passer-by to wash their feet, whether anyone was showering or not. Of course, no one showered unclad. The upside of its openness was the feeling of being at one with nature when exposed to the sky, to forested Mt Tatondong, to buffaloes and to the myriad other rice field residents.

Having just showered while looking up at the mountains and knowing that our help comes from the Lord, Delwyn concluded the same day's journal with reflections on Psalm 121:

*The beautiful promises of the Lord that He will watch over all our comings and goings. My heart is so full of praise to the Lord with the reality of this as experienced on our journey here and in our adjustment to the village again.*

Our host, the minister, Pa' Pandita, whom we called Pua' and the children called Nene', lasted two more days and died on the Friday morning. We moved the three children into our room, leaving their room empty for other visitors. Suddenly there was a whirlwind of activity. Young men were busy chopping firewood. Young women were busy husking and winnowing rice. The rice harvest continued to its conclusion at about 1:00 p.m. Men were sent to cut *pantung*, the largest of the local species of bamboo in order to prop up the house. With potentially 100 people at a time upstairs, there was a very real danger of the house collapsing. Beneath the

*Grieving*

house, in the area where we used to live, work resumed on the coffin. Pa' Pandita had commissioned a large log to be brought down from the forest months ago for his eventual funeral. This had been roughly hollowed and shaped but was some way off being finished. Delwyn was sent downhill to a kiosk to buy some tea. This was an unusual drink in the area, and she wondered why it was suddenly preferred to coffee. On her return she found that it was to be used to wash the body with and to put in the deceased's mouth. Meanwhile, Mama Ondong was inconsolable with grief, wailing loudly and saying how she wanted to follow her father into the grave.

Generally, when someone dies in the Tabulahan area they are buried within 30 hours to obviate the odour of decay. Occasionally this extends to 40 hours to allow family to arrive. Because Pa' Pandita was so widely respected, extra time was given to allow more mourners to come from far away, and it was 56 hours before his body was buried. It had been dressed in several layers of clothing with his ministerial gown being the outer layer. As well as this, a woman from across in Tabulahan performed a ceremony purported to remove odour from the body.

The coffin, once finished and decorated, was so heavy that it was no small feat to get it up the steep stairway and in through the front door. There was renewed wailing and clinging from his daughter as the body was lifted into the coffin and the hinged lid closed and padlocked. The coffin was just as difficult to manhandle down the narrow stairs on the way out, and all but spilled. Once on the ground, long bamboo poles were lashed to it so that a dozen men could carry it the mile or so to its prepared resting place. Esther asked why they were carrying Nene'. We must have answered something along the lines of, "Because he can't walk now that he is dead."

She had a very good follow-up question, "So, why did they

lock him in?" She had other questions after returning from the burial plot.

Members from three congregations came to pay respects to the grieving household later that afternoon. Each held a short service. Following those, in the room where a buffalo was being cut up, away from the cigarette smoke of the front room and the hearth smoke of the kitchen where cauldrons of rice were being cooked, Delwyn and Esther found a space on a bench where they could talk. Esther still had lots of questions, like: "Do strong people die?" Delwyn explained about the difference between a soul and its body and talked of how Jesus was dead (like Nene') for three days but then came back to life and that is why we have hope of living again with him. Esther seemed to realise the seriousness of life and death for the first time and wanted to become a follower of Jesus right then. But with the radio blaring, smoke and dogs drifting in and out, the smell of offal and raw meat and people stepping over legs continually, Delwyn thought it would be best to wait until we retired for the night. That night under the mosquito net, we had the privilege of leading our daughter to the throne-room of God's grace. She was as pleased as we were and happily went to sleep soon after.

Over the course of the next month there was a steady stream of guests coming to pay their respects. Some were whole congregations who also held a memorial service; others were families or individuals. Many stayed all night: the women chatting, the men playing dominoes and smoking. The numbers and hence the thickness of the smoke diminished as the month wore on and we were able to sleep better, but we all developed smokers' coughs. Several of the family also came down with vomiting and diarrhoea, due, we suspect, to unrefrigerated meat being several days past its 'best before date'.

But, for all that, we were able to have some good Scripture-checking sessions with some of the visitors, as well as with others whom we visited in their homes. For one or two of them it took a lot of reassurance that we were not testing *them*, but rather how understandable the *translation* of the passage was for any reader.

In between, Delwyn was teaching the ladies up in Langsa' (and later below in Salu Leäng) two other songs that she had written. Songs were generally taught by writing the tonic-sol-fa numbers on the wall with a piece of chalk. This time we had another tool. We had brought a miniature keyboard with us for the first time, donated by friends. It was powered by flashlight batteries, so was easily portable and, of course, useful in a place without power outlets. Now the children had no excuse for not doing their piano practice while in the village. (On previous trips they had had to use a laminated cardboard keyboard, which, while making no sound whatever, still enabled them to maintain muscle memory for the scales and pieces they had learned. I wonder what went through the minds of their local friends who sometimes watched bemused these strange foreigners tapping soundlessly on black and white rectangles. Hmm.) The keys of the donated keyboard were smaller and fewer than standard, but it was a good tool for teaching choral groups their parts. Äto' had also been singing Delwyn's Psalm 23 at some of the young peoples' groups and we were hearing it frequently.

When not visiting or doing comprehension checking, there was often time available to get out our ancient little Toshiba T1100+ laptop. This was the first computer we ever owned, featuring two 3½ inch floppy drives in lieu of a hard drive—one for a simple editing program, the other for the data being worked on. Its one advantage was that, with no hard drive and no backlighting for the screen, its battery could potentially last up to six hours on a charge. We had a small solar panel that plugged directly into it for charging. Our little T1100+

was getting progressively more temperamental, but we left it in the village for times such as this when we could make use of it for simple data entry. We took no other computer with us. There were days when we were able to do quite a bit of back translating for forthcoming consultant checks. And there were times when the laptop was playing up and was all but unusable. Often prayer resolved the problem after we stupidly had tried everything else we could think of.

So much more happened that trip, too many things to go into details over. There was a runaway member of our host's extended family returning unmarried with a baby, subsequently adopted by Mama Ondong. There was one of our former co-workers tried in a village court in a paternity suit and forced to marry. He then immediately absconded for a year or so. There were the usual times of visiting gravely sick friends and giving medicines and praying. The Gospel of Mark and the book of Genesis were distributed in each of the congregations where it had not been done on our last trip. And there was a wedding, an engagement ceremony, a string of memorials and other church-related events. After several weeks we were tired and looking forward to getting back to the Philippines but were buoyed by God's goodness and reminded of it daily. Delwyn wrote:

> *As I've been reading, I've found a spot behind the house among the rice fields that is quiet and peaceful… I've not been in such a peaceful spot for ages. My heart is full of worship and praise to the Lord for all He has done and as I treasure these psalms, I think of the ones I typed the back-translation for today that one day will be read by people here. I can only pray that God will do what He wants to do in the hearts of all those who read His Word. May I not limit what He can do in my limited thinking.*

## 17

# House to House

Two days after arriving back in Davao we moved house. Other colleagues had gone on furlough, so we took over their rental for the time they were away. It was a smaller place than the previous but was away from busy roads and thus less dusty. It was also closer to the school the boys attended and to the kindergarten Esther was about to enrol in.

A second blessing was the use of a car while yet other colleagues were away for a year. For the past few years, we had got by with public transport, as jeepneys and taxis were both cheap and plentiful. Now that we had the use of a car, it was wonderful to be able to go anywhere without having to walk out to a main road first, especially in torrential rain.

Äto' returned to Davao a few weeks later with another Tabulahan man, Iyä, who came to assist with consultant checks. We had been able to complete comprehension and naturalness checks of *Life of King David*, Revelation, I & II Thessalonians and Philemon while in the village during June and July, and these were all scheduled to be checked with consultants over the coming months. Iyä proved to be a very capable young language assistant, whom we would have welcomed as part of the team going forward. However, he had commitments back home and his skills as a carpenter were in high demand, so it was unlikely that he would be able to return. Fortunately, we had another candidate in the pipeline to work alongside Äto' and me, beginning the following year.

Meanwhile, Delwyn began a new school year of teaching music to grades 1 to 5 and to the kindergarten class. When not doing so, she was busy working on Tabulahan songs based on translated Scripture verses. At about this time Bob Fitts came to Davao to hold a song writing seminar which Delwyn was able to attend. She found it added insight and impetus to her own song writing, particularly to the Tabulahan songs she was working on. Now that *Life of King David* was finalised, including 15 of the psalms attributed to him, she found a few well-loved passages to put music to. Äto' approved the resultant songs, thought some (like Psalm 19) could be longer, and asked for Psalm 103 to be arranged in four-part harmony, as no other Tabulahan scripture song had ever had more than three parts previously. Delwyn felt honoured to be the first person to do so.

> *It was an amazing feeling reading through the selected Psalms of David that we've translated to look for possibilities to put to music. It struck me that I had first choice—no one had gone before me in picking out words to put music to. In English it is hard to find a psalm that hasn't had a song based on it... When I think what my dream is, I am somewhat awed at the privilege before me of writing music for Tabulahan, although it seems so daunting. Yet I pray that the Lord could use these songs to bring the translated Scriptures to life, not just for Tabulahan but for [neighbouring languages] too.*

Christmas followed and Delwyn's mother joined us again for a few weeks. Christmas in the Philippines has its own unique flavour. Shops begin being decorated and Christmas songs begin being played in the department stores as early as August. By December every department is ablaze with coloured lights and dinky tunes. It is not uncommon to hear a dozen different tunes sounding simultaneously from a dozen Christmas tree lights in a store. Sometimes the seasonal messages are a bit mixed. In one shopping mall there were Christmas decorations featuring a suspended six-foot Styrofoam angel, decorated with Christmas lights and holding up a banner saying, 'Santa Claus is coming to town'. Groups of carollers called at the gate nightly singing a verse or two of any Christmas song, before launching into 'We Wish You a Merry Christmas' and concluding with several loud greetings of "Mayong Pasko!" For a couple of years Esther thought this meant "Give us money!" instead of its actual meaning: "Merry Christmas!" It was certainly the cue for us to take something out to them. New Year celebrations there were also something special. So loud were the explosions from fireworks and gunshots that year, that the two rabbits we gave to the boys for Christmas died of shock on New Year's Eve.

Äto' and Iyä had returned to Indonesia for Christmas—Iyä heading back to the village to continue his carpentry; Äto' spending time in Manado where he could link up with Uja, our new co-translator. Uja was the adopted son of the late minister, our host in Salu Leäng. We had observed him growing up from our first days there and had always been impressed with his work ethic and character. Both his natural father and his adoptive family were pleased that we were keen to have him work on the translation with us.

So, in early February I went to the airport to pick up Uja and Äto', for whom international flights were now no big deal. However, there was some irregularity with Uja's paperwork, apparently, and the airport authorities were about to send him straight back to Indonesia. Äto' came out to tell me what was going on and eventually security guards allowed me to enter as an interpreter, as neither Äto' nor Uja could communicate such matters in English. I pleaded Uja's case and in the end the immigration officials released him to my care, provided we sorted it out with the immigration office in town next day. It turned out to be a minor matter and Uja was permitted to stay. In retrospect, we saw this as yet another unsubtle attempt by the powers of darkness to hinder the spread of the light. Uja proved to be a worthy member of the translation team, and he continued in the task until the New Testament was eventually completed. Subsequently both Äto' and Uja completed degrees in theology.

One day, after their weekly English class, the two men returned with some of the most meaningful spiritual questions we had ever heard from Tabulahan speakers, questions like: "How can you be sure you are going to heaven?" This led to some in depth discussions and prayer times, and a new level of honesty and openness about their own spiritual needs and those of their community. It was the first time Tabulahan speakers had acknowledged to us the spiritual fear their families live under. They asked us to pray specifically against this and for the salvation of the people of their community. It was a hallelujah moment, and the best of birthday presents for Delwyn.

> *The highlight of the day was having Äto' and Uja come back from [their English class] asking about salvation… it almost seems as though the blinders have come off and they really want to know the Lord in a deeper way… We prayed with them and encouraged them to ask questions any time they wanted to about anything. This is the most meaningful discussion we have ever had with anyone from Tabulahan and we pray it will not be the last. Thank You,*

*Lord, for an absolutely incredible birthday! Together with yesterday's tears in the worship time and today's tears of joy, it has been so good—an almost intoxicating feeling of gratitude and praise.*

A few months earlier, Delwyn had again been asked to put on some sort of school production for Christmas. "T is for Christmas" went down well. It was more a themed variety show than a musical *per se*, as she had formerly produced. Now with the school year winding down, Delwyn was again looking at writing a musical as a year-end production. Our three children had always enjoyed the story *The Selfish Giant*, and I always got a bit misty-eyed by the end when reading it to them. So, in our evenings, after working on the translation and school teaching through the day, we collaborated on a script, lyrics and music towards that goal.* We had some wonderful adult helpers with skills in sets, costumes, makeup, lighting, etc., and more than 70 energetic children in the cast and choir. However, moving to a new house the week of the performance is not to be recommended!

Finding a house to rent had itself been a little stressful. Our colleagues whose house we were presently occupying were due to return, and house hunting happened to coincide with government elections. This last fact might not seem significant, but 'to let' notices and other 'classifieds' were generally nailed up on power poles. During the build-up to elections, the power poles and walls of the city became festooned with election posters, making it difficult to see any classifieds at all, let alone the 'House for Rent' signs we sought. Finally, though, we found a very suitable place, close to the school

---

* See song: "Wounds of Love" (one of the songs from *The Selfish Giant*)

and SIL office and within our budget. It had its quirks, like being not the only number 6 in a street with non-consecutive numbering. It had its drawbacks too as we were to find out later, but it met our family's needs well. Beyond these, it also had a room for Äto' and Uja and a work room for translation and language-related activities. It was a real blessing and was to be our home base for the next six years.

Two weeks after moving house and putting on *The Selfish Giant* musical, it was time once more to return to Indonesia for two months to continue the checking of material translated. It turned out to be one of our more difficult village visits, due largely to extremely muddy conditions and a run of poor health. Each of us in turn had combinations of fever, sore throats, headaches, nausea, vomiting, diarrhoea and lethargy that lasted weeks. I also had a swollen knee, making it difficult to bend my leg for a week, and a fishbone stuck in my throat for a couple of days that I could have done without. It was a rare Tuesday that we were all able to go across to Tabulahan for the weekly market—often a parent and child went while the other parent stayed home sick with the other sick children. One week the two boys went on behalf of their sick parents and sister.

The other factor that made this a difficult trip was a change in economic conditions. The Asian monetary crisis had hit, such that the Indonesian rupiah had followed the Thai baht, the Korean won, and other currencies in devaluing. This meant that coffee and cacao prices reached record highs and every available villager was picking and processing cash crops like never before. Hence, it was a very difficult time to find checkers for the portions we had been working on. However, in the end we did find a few people who were also too unwell for manual work, but able to read with us and answer questions. Before we left, we were able to complete comprehension checks on Romans, I, II & III John, James and part of John's Gospel. We also saw the newly published book of Acts distributed.

We were so run down that for the first time ever we longed to get back to the city and even curtailed our time in the village. Rather than walk all the way to Lakähäng in one day, we decided to spend all day Sunday in Tabulahan with our former hosts, thus shortening the next day's journey and also affording us the opportunity to attend church with the Tabulahan congregation. With the path being so muddy, the 40-minute trip across the valley took us two hours, with little time to rinse the mud off before the morning service began. In the afternoon we attended the ladies' meeting and were encouraged that Mama Maya, recently made a deacon, was not only sharing at the meeting, but was basing her homily on the as yet unpublished Tabulahan Romans which she had been checking for naturalness.

The journey back to the city was slow but largely uneventful, apart from an hour delay while the bus tried several times to get up a particularly muddy hill. Once back in Ujung Pandang, friends there suggested we take a few days to recover in a nice hotel, given that with the new exchange rate there had never been a cheaper time to play the tourist. It was a very relaxing four days in the nicest hotel we have ever stayed in, complete with swimming pool and gym. Poor Delwyn stayed in bed the whole time and couldn't eat much of the delicious Indonesian cuisine we all love. She arrived back in Davao seven kilos lighter than she had been two months earlier but continued to experience weariness for several weeks. She did not recommend the illness as a slimming method.

Gradually things got back to normal, and we settled into our lovely new abode. As well as having all the rooms we required and a high ceiling that kept it moderately cool, the house had a small garden out front with a good-sized chico tree just begging to be the bearer of a kids' play-deck-cum-treehouse. So, for a couple of days Isaac and his dad worked on its construction and the rope ladder to reach it. Isaac wanted to know why we were making a rope ladder when there was a perfectly good, barbed wire fence to climb up! Fraser, who was climbing Mt Apo at the time with a group of friends, missed out on its construction but enjoyed it thereafter, as did Esther. Delwyn's favourite part of the house was a covered area underneath our bedroom—a tranquil spot for a quiet time with the Lord, or for a morning tea discussion with the men on whichever passage we had been working on.

Delwyn became slightly less enamoured with the house one morning when she opened one of the less-used built-in cupboards in our bedroom, only to be met with a writhing mass of termites devouring all the paper and cardboard the cupboard contained. This was the third house in Davao where we had encountered the industrious little critters munching their way through everything. Exterminators were called in.

But it was something else that made us realise how this lovely house came to fall within our budget. The first time it rained like only a tropical setting in wet season knows how to rain, the street filled, the front garden flooded and incrementally the deluge inched up the foundations. We stuffed towels under the front and back doors to no avail. By the time it was several inches higher, the water was streaming in, crossing the floor and soaking into the plywood partition walls through which the termites had made their way. Fraser and Isaac's bedroom was more than a foot lower than the rest of downstairs and became an indoor pool. Everything on low shelves had to be elevated to a higher plane. And we switched off power at the mains to avoid a short or something worse. Next morning we spent a few hours draining the boys' room and cleaning up the silt. For days afterwards there was a damp sewage smell from overflowing septic tanks.

This was the pattern several times a year. Sometimes we were sitting around the dining table ankle deep in water. Sometimes the boys' bamboo beds floated. Dozens of wooden parquet floor tiles would lift and float around the room, occasionally becoming life rafts for rodents! At least the water was not cold. The upside was that we could catch fish in the street, and sometimes even in the garden. Muddy fish like snakehead and climbing perch may not be exactly gourmet fare, but our hunter-gatherer children ate them, nonetheless.

During the next four months we had a run of Kiwi visitors. Visitors were always welcome, but it was especially nice to be able to speak New Zealand English and drop our post-vocalic Rs (which we cultivated to be betteR undeRstood by noRth American colleagues and Filipino neighbouRs alike). And of course, visitors from home often brought special treats like cheddar cheese and Vegemite! Ian Vail was the NZ Wycliffe director at the time and also a former colleague on the field in Indonesia. It was great to catch up with him for a few days.

Next, my brother and his family joined us for two and a half weeks. Last time they visited, there were just the two of them, the only family members ever to make it to Tabulahan. Now they had been joined by their three lovely children, all born since Esther arrived. We spent some quality family time with them, visiting a couple of day trip beauty spots and a few days in our favourite holiday getaway at Nasuli. I enjoyed their stay so much that when they left I was miserable for weeks. I can honestly say it was the only time I ever felt really homesick in all the years we were away. But that was a small price to pay for the joy of having family around.

Delwyn's mother was our most frequent visitor and we looked forward to her return for Christmas. Before that, though, we enjoyed an overnight visit from our friends the Hunts, who were returning from New Zealand en route to their village home in Sinuda and home base in Nasuli. They often stopped at our place when passing through and were the most easy-going of guests, happy to spread out on the floor with their half a dozen children.

It was about the time of all the visitors that our computer hard drive crashed. Äto' had begun his theological training and Uja was also still in Indonesia, so I had spent the past month or so working on the Tabulahan dictionary and some time on key term and logical connector databases. All of this was backed up on a tape drive I had purchased from a colleague, so I was not worried initially. Then I discovered that the tape drive was corrupted and almost none of the recent data was recoverable. In addition to my lost Tabulahan data, Delwyn had lost almost all of her orchestration work on the songs she had written for *The Selfish Giant*, and also any recent correspondence. Furthermore, the music program she had been using could no longer interface with the keyboard, and the sounds coming from the sound card were no longer right. It was not one of our better moments.

However, good things can come out of bad situations. After replacing the hard drive, I found that it was still under guarantee in the USA where it was made. A colleague was going there and kindly arranged for and brought back a replacement, along with a very good backup program. So, we now had two hard drives, one easily removable, and a far better backup system. Delwyn asked her mother to see if she could bring a Roland sound card when she came, which we knew to be expensive, as quality often costs. The day she purchased it, however, it was on sale at less than 15 percent of the normal price! Once installed, everything connected with the music program started working again and with better sounds than ever.

Delwyn progressively reworked her lost orchestrations while I progressively reworked the lost dictionary entries, and both of us felt we had done a better job the second time around. The only lost translation data was several chapters of John's Gospel. But, as we had a printout, it only needed to be retyped. Delwyn's mother once again came to the rescue during her Christmas visit.

From February to April Uja worked with me on drafting Galatians and Hebrews and on revising an old draft of Colossians. After that we both attended a translation workshop in Manado put on by the Indonesian Bible Society. While there we were able to do some checking and also see to the publication of a six-epistle volume (Romans, I & II Timothy, I & II Thessalonians, James). Then, while I returned to the Philippines to work on back translations, Uja headed south to the village area to see to the volume's distribution and to do further checking and conferring with reviewers.

There was also plenty of new drafting to look forward to working on later in the year when Uja returned. But first we were to have a rather unusual summer break.

## 18

# New Songs

Delwyn was becoming ever more interested in ethnomusicology—not for its own sake, but with a view to making worship relevant in the context of the culture we were so involved with. Someone else was putting on school musicals that year, so there was more time available for Delwyn to do some research. She read every ethnomusicology book and every ethnomusicology journal she could get her hands on. Still, however, she felt she would benefit greatly from getting a solid course on the subject under her belt.

A five-week course was on offer in the middle of the year. The downside was that it was to take place in Texas. Dallas is far from being close to Davao. We would need to find funds from somewhere. Also, the thought of Delwyn being away for five and a half weeks was not at all appealing to me. I'm sorry to write that I was more a party pooper than positive, but eventually realised how important it was for Delwyn and backed her in these plans.

We still were unsure about how we could afford not only the course costs, but also Delwyn's trip to the USA. Then we heard that some funds might be available for travel, as expertise gained would be of benefit to the wider group. We prayed about this and about the rest of the money needed. Then out of the blue a wealthy donor decided to give $1,000 to each translation team around the world to use where needed!

Wow! It was just what we lacked to cover the course costs, and Delwyn was on her way.

The course was scheduled for June-July, during which the children were off school for their long summer break. At that time of year, we would normally be in the villages of Tabulahan checking translated materials. However, because of sectarian violence in parts of Indonesia, including Sulawesi, we were restricted from going there at this time, so the Dallas course in no way impeded our translation work schedule. We figured we could still make a trip to Tabulahan in December for checking purposes or, if that would not work out, then the following January when the boys would be away at an outdoor education program, and Esther could potentially board with friends. But right now, the children had five and a half motherless weeks of summer vacation and just a stay-at-home dad to entertain them.

We decided to make some home videos—a surprise for Mum's return. Brainstorming for ideas, we settled on making a series of spoof advertisements, based on old New Zealand television ads that Mum might remember. Then we decided to film a five minute 'epic'—our take on Hannibal crossing the Alps, but with two Hannibals (Fraser and Isaac), Esther as an elephant, and Pepper, the rabbit, as a kangaroo. We had no editing software—everything had to be shot sequentially and in a single take. Retakes led to some terrible edits (which we left in). Needless to say, none of these would be box-office successes, nor win any accolades with film societies, but we had a lot of laughs and thus survived the summer.

Meanwhile Delwyn spent her weeks learning about recording and analysing musical systems outside the norms of western melody, harmony and rhythm. She found it stretching but invigorating, especially as she had the Tabulahan musical context in mind, rather than studying in a vacuum. Though she was missing family, she made some good friends among the staff and students, and there were a few familiar faces from the Indonesia branch around the SIL centre in Dallas to make her feel less homesick. The tutors had all worked extensively as ethnomusicologists in different parts of the world, including Asia, Africa and South America.

Delwyn wrote:

> *I heard story after story of the effectiveness of using the musical heart language in a culture to worship God and express biblical truth. One that touched me was about a young woman who was a refugee from her country living in the USA. She was gifted in using her traditional music system and, after coming to know Jesus, she spent a year composing a 45-minute song on Genesis 1-11. When she returned to her country, she sang this song among many unbelievers who flocked to hear her sing because of the appeal their own style of music held for them.*

After the conclusion of the course, while still in North America, Delwyn was able to spend a day catching up with Ava, a friend in Seattle whom we knew from our time in Palu and Davao, and then another day with Lisa, an old high school friend just over the Canadian border. Finally, she recrossed the Pacific to her long awaiting brood. Besides the home movies, we had another surprise for Mum's arrival. Esther was sporting a bright green cast from her wrist to up past her elbow. Parents grow through trauma. This is the reason jungle gyms were invented.

Once back in Davao, Delwyn worked on a closer analysis of traditional Tabulahan songs to see if writing in their traditional style would help in communicating the written Word. Knowing that the traditional style may not prove so popular with younger people, she tried writing in a variety of musical styles to see which ones really reached their hearts.*

At the same time, she was introducing these concepts to any other Indonesian men currently working with our colleagues in Davao in order to get them thinking about how they might foster indigenous worship in their own language groups. Several of them picked up the challenge, keen to rediscover the marginalised music of their culture. One man remarked that it was not that the missionaries of previous generations forbade the use of their music, it was that the community liked the new music brought in, not realising that they might forget their own music in the process.

While Delwyn was enjoying putting all she had learned into practice, she was experiencing some distracting health issues. She felt a great deal of discomfort in her hip that made it difficult to sit for any length of time, and her fingers were painful enough to make piano playing more a pain than a pleasure. She was also needing some surgery but felt she would rather delay that until we returned to New Zealand the following year. In the meantime, she mourned the passing of her dear Aunty Beryl, glad for all the wonderful memories she had shared with her aunt and cousins, but sorrowful that she could not be there with family members at that time. It was a difficult end to the millennium.

The year 2000. We remember it well: worldwide angst that computers would crash, planes fall from the sky and civilisation as we knew it would come to an end. Fortunately, the dawning of the new millennium saw none of that. For those of us in Davao that particular midnight brought in the usual cacophony of firecrackers and gunshots, but also a respectable display of more colourful pyrotechnics across the neighbour-

---

* See song: '2 Tesalonika 3:16'

hood that Delwyn said equalled any she had seen in Dallas on July 4th! A new year—more than that, a new millennium! What an opportunity for new beginnings and for renewal of commitment.

We had had a quiet Christmas. Gran had not come this year, so our children had to make do with very few presents. In fact, it was the children's idea to make a donation to a local orphanage and minimise what we gave to each other. We did, however, buy a two-man tent.

Davao lies in the shadow of Mt Apo, a semi-active volcano and, at almost 3,000 metres (9,692 feet), the Philippines' highest mountain. As such it is a favourite climb of local groups and a few tourists. Fraser had already climbed it a couple of times with friends, sharing a tent in the process. There was another trip planned for early January and this time Isaac and Dad were going too. We figured the three of us could squeeze into a two-man tent, especially as Fraser and three others had spent the night at the very summit with only a single rain poncho over them last time. In bitterly cold rain.

After climbing a steep trail for most of the first day, we came out of the forest onto a plateau of thick moss surrounded by slender, stunted trees. It reminded me of certain alpine meadows and also of parts of south Westland back home. We pitched tents at Lake Venado from which next day we could easily climb to the summit and return within a few hours. Camping had always been one of my fondest childhood memories. It felt good to be building similar memories with the next generation. After two nights at the campsite and a short stint at the summit viewing Davao in the distance between grey-white flocks of swiftly passing clouds, we returned to our starting point, Lake Agco, where most of us got into the turbid water of the hot springs. Aaah!

On the return journey our collective good humour evaporated. Through the open windows of the jeepney, we were stunned to see the aftermath of an horrific accident. A motorised tricab had collided with something and burst into flames. The incinerated bodies of the passengers were still smouldering as they lay on the road next to the smoking tricab. This was a mode of transport we had frequently taken. It was very sobering for all of us and an instant reminder of our own mortality.

Perhaps, along with starting a new millennium, this was instrumental in our family's rekindled desire to see God working among the Tabulahan and Aralle people. We confessed that we had often been neglectful in praying earnestly for them and began afresh. Later that month Delwyn wrote:

> *What an amazing privilege we have that we are working not for food that spoils, but for the food (the Word of God) that endures to eternal life. My heart is full of love to the Lord that He has called us and that He has renewed our sense of vision in recent weeks. My thoughts often turn to Tabulahan, and more and more as I lift my feeble prayers to Him, I want to pray even more. Thank You, Jesus! It's so neat to see how the kids are praying more fervently and from their hearts for the Tabulahan people too.*

Once a year the middle-schoolers went somewhere in the Philippines for a week of 'Outdoor Ed.' This sometimes involved visiting an historic site, like Corregidor. Sometimes there was more of an emphasis on learning survival skills (like making fire without matches in order to cook small bats in bamboo tubes for supper!) In addition, there was always some practical help given to the local community. This year Fraser and Isaac were both in middle school and so were able to enjoy Outdoor Ed. together. This would coincide with a week of our time away. Delwyn and I were planning a three-week trip to the villages of Tabulahan since we had missed going the previous summer. We hoped to also visit Kinätäng, a village we had never seen, as it was outside the main area and off a side road we never traversed. Good friends were happy to have Esther board with them for this time, and other friends looked after the boys during the time when Outdoor Ed. was not being held.

On previous trips we had waited until reaching Ujung Pandang before getting materials printed there. This time we thought we could get the printing process for *Life of King David* and some riddle books started in Manado, and then Uja could follow us from there with the books when they were ready. We found a print shop whose proprietor was more than helpful. He refused to charge us extra for a rush job and we headed to the airport (with Uja) after waiting just a day. Unfortunately, the airline cancelled the flight. Amazingly, they put us up in a hotel for the night—the only time of many such occasions. The one positive was that we were able to be of assistance to a distraught German couple who needed to pick up luggage left in Ujung Pandang in time to connect with an international flight. We said we would be praying for them. "How can I believe in a God if we have to miss our international flight because of this?" the young woman complained. A phone call to Tim and Barbara later and we were able to assure the German couple that our good friends in Ujung Pandang would pick up their baggage and bring it to the airport as they passed through. This they did with a glad heart.

After spending some hours of good fellowship with our friends, we caught an unusually quiet night bus to Mamuju with no radio or video blaring. Next morning, we caught a minivan to Le'beng that needed a wheel change en route. And after only a couple of hours there we were able to catch a small bus to Lakähäng. Those two hours gave us time to have a bit of breakfast and chat to some Tabulahan folk resident in Le'beng. A couple of new bridges made this next leg of the journey, that had been fraught with incidents in the past, take less than an hour! On arrival at Lakähäng we trusted the Lord to provide a vehicle should it be His will that we still make it to Kinätäng that day. He did and so we were delighted that, although there had been unforeseen delays, He still had His hand on our travels, and we were back on schedule. Iyä decided that he would accompany us from Lakähäng, as Uja, like us, was unfamiliar with the route.

Kinätäng was a relatively new village many kilometres downstream from the main Tabulahan area. It had been settled in recent years by some pioneering Tabulahan families who carved out plots for housing, rice fields and gardens from the forest. The neighbouring villages upstream and downstream spoke the Makki language.

Half an hour after leaving Lakähäng we hopped off the back of a truck at a point where a narrow suspension bridge spanned the wide Bonehau river. It was beginning to rain, but not yet heavily. Still, it made the path through bush and cacao groves slippery, and after an hour it was pouring. We arrived saturated but joyful that we had finally made it to this out of the way village that we had long wanted to reach. And we felt at home immediately in the company of wonderful hosts who knew of us, and others we had previously met in the Tabulahan heartland. It was durian season, so, as well as the very welcome coffee to warm us, there was plenty of that wonderful spiky fruit, described as 'hell on the outside, heaven within'. If you have never tried it, let me just say that it has the ability to warm you repeatedly. I have heard its consistency described as cream cheese, its flavour described as somewhere between onion, kerosene and vomit, and its smell, well, never mind. It is an acquired taste—not Delwyn's favourite—especially when over-ripe. These were perfect—just ripe.

The next day was Sunday, our 18th anniversary. Interestingly, it was also 18 years since this village came into being. We trooped off across the soccer field between the grazing cattle and up the slight incline to the church. Following half an hour of notices in which we were welcomed, the service began, in which we were more formally welcomed, and it was getting embarrassing during prayers that we were still being welcomed! We were asked to sing, as usual. This gave opportunity to introduce one of the six new songs Delwyn had composed to bring with us. At the end of the service, an elder announced that the ladies should all come over to the house where we were staying later in the afternoon so that Mama Fraser could teach them all some new songs.

They did and she did. Songs are generally taught by writing the lyrics and accompanying numerical note system on an available wall with a piece of chalk. Some of the songs Delwyn had composed had multiple parts, so the front room walls were soon festooned with numbers, dashes and lyrics. Our hosts were quite happy to have this graffiti temporarily besmirch their living room. I, who read music not at all, was impressed by how quickly the ladies picked up all the various parts after just a couple of runs through.

Even after the ladies dispersed, the music continued. Most teenage boys in the area know a few guitar chords, so Delwyn also showed those who were hanging around how they could accompany a couple of the more contemporary songs on a guitar. And then there were the mini xylophones that appeared that afternoon. These they called *kulintang*, which generally across insular southeast Asia refers to a series of brass gongs but can also be used of xylophone orchestras. These locally made versions were much smaller and had been made of strips of split bamboo across a wooden frame. And now they were sounding out rhythmically and in simple harmonies, filling the house with music. It was wonderful.

No one there knew it was a special occasion for us, but that evening we were treated to a very special and most memorable anniversary dinner. Uja and Iyä had gone visiting that evening, so the two of us were to eat alone. (Guests typically are served before household members.) The table was set with several dishes: beautifully tender wild pork, pumpkin in coconut cream, greens, noodles and rice—an absolute banquet! Soft romantic lighting was provided from the glow of the kitchen hearth and a lamp in the doorway. We were serenaded by gentle *kulintang* music emanating from the front room to the accompaniment of two dogs howling through the kitchen wall. Then there was the cat, dressed in black with white bib, who waited on our table. Literally. I lost count of the times we shoved him off, but he was most persistent, expecting a tip as waiters sometimes do. It was, perhaps, our most memorable anniversary ever.

After we had retraced our steps to Lakähäng (part of which involved sitting in the back of a pickup truck on a pile of durians—not to be recommended), we caught up with our first village hostess, Mama Tahe', whom we had heard was recently widowed. We grieved with her for our dear friend. Her youngest, So'yang, was with her and told us that Papa Tahe' used to read regularly at night from the Tabulahan publications of Genesis and Mark. This touched our hearts, especially as we remembered how he had once told us that if we wrote 'r' as most people wanted it written, instead of 'd', he would never buy one of our books! Staying in Lakähäng that night gave us opportunity to meet up with the head of the congregation there and share with him and others the six new songs we had brought. Everyone seemed to appreciate them, although some indicated that they would have liked one or two of them to be a bit longer.

Once in the main Tabulahan area we found the same receptivity to the new songs wherever we shared them, leaving printed copies and a cassette for song leaders to teach their groups. On such a visit to Langsa' we discovered that a new hamlet had been formed. Worried by the threat of landslides in this steep village, several families had rebuilt their houses along a narrow ridge further around the side of the hill. The new village was named 'Lisu'. We visited folk in several of the houses. Some we already knew, others invited us to see their new, sometimes partially finished, dwellings.

One such was one of Uja's aunts. She asked us if we would like to visit her next-door neighbours and name the newborn. Delwyn wrote:

*It always seems like such an unasked-for honour. What right have we to name someone else's baby?! Rahe', the young mother, was holding her baby as we came in. He was only two weeks old and ever so tiny still. Robin thought 'Yosua' (Joshua) would be a good name for this first born— a pioneer of this new land. They were happy with that choice, and we explained that Joshua was whole-hearted before the Lord and went bravely into the new land. Then we sang one of the songs we had written as a blessing and prayed with them. Somehow, I felt I was on holy ground with it all—such a privilege to share with these folk in a way they clearly appreciated.*

Though it was one of our shorter trips to the village, the Lord arranged for us to achieve more than we were hoping for. Looking back, we can see how many times that was the case. This time we were able to see the newly printed *Life of King David* distributed, as well as previous Bible portions that had not yet been distributed, complete village checks of Ephesians and Philippians, give each congregation some Bible verse colouring books for Sunday school prizes and teach the six new songs, leaving written music and a cassette with each congregation.

One more thing on this trip was to give out little riddle books. These two booklets were the result of a number of riddle-collecting conversations over several years, some while sitting up through the night with a house full of men as we prepared *balun dakang* (rice bars cooked in leaves) for the following day's wedding. Here are some samples: 'If only one or two, I'm afraid; if many, I'm not afraid.'\* 'Take me and I will take for you.'\*\* 'A pregnant woman walking backwards.'\*\*\* After collecting more than 70 riddles, we prepared these two little books. And now they were presented to eager children, who loved to puzzle over each clue before turning the page to see its answer with accompanying picture. Little did they know they were practising reading their own language with each one.

The trip back to the Philippines was uneventful, apart from missing a night bus by minutes, having the next day's morning bus cancelled, avoiding the 1:00 p.m. bus in favour of the 3:00 p.m. bus (and then passing the 1:00 p.m. bus stuck in a ditch!), missing the next day's flight to Manado (because I misread the tickets), catching the next day's flight but not quite in time to catch our international flight to Davao, and spending three extra days in Manado to await the next one. Needless to say, it made our reunion with three special young people all the sweeter.

\* Floorboards
\*\* Tongs
\*\*\* Calf (of leg)

## 19

# Everywhere Has Its Challenges

With another field term drawing to a close and the prospect of home assignment intruding on our thoughts, we tried to make the most of these final few months. While in Tabulahan in January, we had been hoping for Iyä to return to assist with consultant checks of John, Hebrews, Ephesians and Philippians. However, he was unable to come. And when another young man, Pe'u', agreed to come in his stead, we thought the problem solved. He travelled with us to Ujung Pandang to get his passport sorted but was immediately sent back to the village to retrieve some paperwork he needed. Subsequent to that, he was again sent back to the village for yet more paperwork and in the end decided not to come.

Our unexpected extra three days waiting in Manado for a flight back to the Philippines afforded us the opportunity of spending more time with Äto', who was enjoying his theological studies in nearby Tomohon. We didn't know it at the time, but he would be the solution to the need for the missing Tabulahan speaker to assist with checks. In a year's time he would be able to take some time off his studies and come to the Philippines to assist with some consultant checks of books he had not been involved in translating.

Meanwhile there were plenty of other things to work on. We needed to keyboard changes following village comprehension and naturalness checks, revise the spelling for certain words in many files, and give some preparatory thought to the 20 percent of the New Testament still either in basic draft form, or not yet begun.

Davao was in the news several times during those months. As well as sectarian violence and kidnapping escalating in other parts of the island of Mindanao that kept us confined to areas close to home, there were incidents within the city proper. Most expatriates working in Davao avoided crowded places and going out in general until things settled down. And then there was the crash of a Boeing 737 on nearby Samal Island as it approached Davao airport with the loss of all 120 people on board. Finally, there was a deranged individual who tried to hijack another 737 between Davao and Manila. It was reported that after discharging a firearm inside the cabin, he demanded to be returned to Davao or else he would detonate the grenade in his hand—he had already removed the pin! Aircrew convinced him that there was not enough fuel to go that far, so he asked for a collection to be taken up from the passengers and for the door to be opened, as he was wearing a (homemade) parachute. The plane descended to 6,000 ft so that the door could be safely opened. According to one of our children's teachers on board the aircraft, he hesitated in the doorway and so was assisted on his way by a member of the aircrew. Apparently, the 'chute partially opened, but the hijacker died on impact, semi-buried in mudflats.

Those few months were unusually wet, with three major street floods finding their way into our house. The worst of these was on Good Friday. Most of this rain had fallen the night before, so as usual we had lifted things from low-lying positions before heading to bed. At 10:00 p.m. we went down to the kitchen to get a drink and found the water already crossing the kitchen and living room floors and getting close to the level of the office floor and that of Uja's room. While Delwyn rearranged Isaac and Uja upstairs in Esther's room and Fraser in our room, I went outside to rescue the rabbit, which I found halfway up a bush and resembling a drowned rat. He spent the night high and dry in the house. Esther slept through the entire procedure and was quite surprised in the morning to find a thick wall to wall silt carpet downstairs that had not been there the day before. A couple of colleagues helped us with the clean-up, including emptying the 16 inches of water remaining in the boys' room.

That evening, as the house continued to dry out, our friends who had helped with the clean-up invited us over to watch a video about a dog sled competition. As it had been taped off TV, there were program promo ads between parts of the movie, including one about life after death. This clearly touched Isaac. Delwyn wrote that night:

*When we were putting the kids to bed, Isaac suddenly burst in the room wanting to recommit his life to the Lord because he was challenged by the promo he had seen. With tears streaming down his face, he prayed a truly heart-led prayer, telling the Lord he wanted to follow him for ever and ever and ever.*

*Esther too was touched by the [movie] story and was sad about the boy's dad dying, so it was good to talk about how the Lord helped me when my dad died...Later she prayed for the families of those who had died in the [Davao] plane crash, realising it would be a sad time for them.*

*Fraser too had been touched by the message of the Cross at 'Crosswalk' [youth group] tonight, and it was neat to see him supporting Isaac tonight and sharing what he'd learned about the different witnesses to Jesus' death. Thank You, Lord, for touching our kids by your Spirit.*

We all need fresh touches from the Spirit of God. Missionaries are no exception. Sometimes members of home churches put their missionaries on a pedestal, as though they live on a higher spiritual plane, always hearing from the Lord and acting on it. In reality, we are all wilful sheep—sometimes following the Shepherd, often wandering off in the opposite direction. Jonah is such a good example of this.

Following on from the school production of *The Selfish Giant*, we thought that perhaps the story of Jonah would be good to cast as a musical. Not only is it a great story, full of action that we were sure the children would love, but also a reminder to all of us in the missionary community that we need to not only hear the Word of the Lord, but act on it as He leads, and be motivated by His compassion for the lost.* We decided to call it *Hey, Joe!*, the greeting given to every Caucasian walking along a street in the Philippines. All of the children played their parts well and Fraser did a great job as 'Joe'. The only disappointing thing was that the boy playing the king of Nineveh was too sick to perform. Consequently, I had to stand in for him as we had no understudies.

\*\*\*\*

Three weeks later our field term had come to an end, and we were once more back in New Zealand. It was nice to be home again, but there were surprises that made life difficult. The first of these was discovering that Delwyn's driver's licence was no longer valid. Changes had been made to driver's licence length of tenure over the years of our absence. The former 'lifetime licences' had been commuted to ten years and Delwyn's had not been converted within the allowable time period. This

---

\* See song: 'Dying To Save' (one of the songs from *Hey, Joe!*)

meant she would have to re-sit everything like a first-time driver. And in the weeks leading up to her practical test, she would only be allowed to drive with a licenced driver next to her. How ridiculous. She had been a good driver for 25 years. She felt quite traumatised by the whole experience. Once she had passed the eye test, the written and the hour-long practical, she was informed that a mistake had been made and she should not have had to go through all this rigmarole. She could therefore fill in some forms and apply for a refund. A little later the agency phoned her to say that, in fact, there was no mistake, and she would not be eligible for a refund. After more phone calls to department heads, it turned out that they had just had a policy change and no, she didn't have to sit, and yes, she was eligible for a refund. Oh, the joys of bureaucracy.

The second surprise led to *me* not driving for a while. I was in the middle of some house renovations, specifically putting in a larger replacement window. As I was cutting some wooden spacers for this, my left thumb drifted too close to the spinning table saw blade, which rather chewed it up. The first doctor to examine it thought it would have to be amputated. However, a specialist in hand surgery was available at the main hospital and operated on it the following day, reconnecting tendon and blood vessels, then grafting skin from the other side of my palm. There followed four weeks in a cast and six weeks of physiotherapy sessions to get a good range of movement back. We were so blessed by the wonderful skills of the whole team. Thank You, Lord! By Christmas I was back driving again. Meanwhile Fraser had also had fingers crushed in the hinges of the school gate, necessitating a quick trip to the hospital.

Christmas came and went with the children involved in the Christmas morning service. The following day we headed north en route to Auckland where we were to be on staff at an

SIL course at the Bible College of New Zealand (now Laidlaw College). We left with plenty of time to catch the ferry across Cook Strait, but an hour before reaching the terminal we were stopped, along with other motorists, due to a large grass fire spanning the road ahead. It would be some hours before we would be able to get through, we were told. In the end we had to overnight in the car. At least Delwyn and the children did. I found it easier sleeping on the road. And we thought this sort of thing only happened on the way to Tabulahan!

We thoroughly enjoyed being back at BCNZ, where we had been studying when Fraser was born, and being back on staff for an SIL course—Delwyn as course coordinator, while I was tutoring in language learning and anthropology. The two boys found ways to be useful around the place: helping in the kitchen, and so on. We enrolled Esther in a local school for the short duration. Auckland is a bit more cosmopolitan than Christchurch, and it was interesting to note that Esther was the only European in the class, not that *she* noticed.

Once back in Christchurch with all three children back in school, Delwyn was able to catch up on neglected correspondence and domestic routines, while I focused on translation-related activities, and we both were involved in some missions-related church events. At the same time there were some medical procedures and other health concerns to attend to.

Easter came and with it a welcome family break near Abel Tasman National Park and at Lake Rotoroa in the Nelson Lakes National Park. Highlights included long walks, picking bags of field mushrooms (enough to share with other campers and make a big pot of delicious soup), enjoyable but fruitless hours of trying to tempt reluctant trout, and hilarious games of Pictionary in the tent. ("Oh, it's a sumo wrestler. I get it now. But his legs sure look like peanuts to me.")

*Everywhere Has Its Challenges*

We shared mixed feelings in the weeks leading up to our return to the Philippines. We had enjoyed the relative normalcy of life in our homeland but were keen to get back to continue the translation work in a setting more conducive to that. It had been an eventful and memorable home assignment, and we now had at least a preliminary draft of the Tabulahan New Testament. At the same time, we were conscious that some of our close friends would no longer be operating from Davao any longer, but rather basing out of their home countries—a small grief for us, but felt, nonetheless. Also, although we knew life in New Zealand to be generally easier than our experience in insular southeast Asia, the lack of spiritual awareness in the West made it a dark place too, with many needs. Delwyn's journal relates some of these feelings:

> *As I read tonight about the families leaving Davao, I grieve again for the different Davao we will return to… With the fact of our return looming, I sometimes wish I could just run away from it all and live a 'normal' life. Sometimes I want to spend more time on song writing and inputting into the lives of other song writers. And sometimes I want to go out and shake the world around me when I see how lost and lonely everyone is. You see it in their faces as they walk down the street… I really love Jesus and want to draw nearer to Him in everything I do, so that all the moments of my day are offered up to Him, not just the times when I feel good. I'm so grateful for such a wonderful family. I'm so proud of them all and how each has special attributes that make them stand out from others. I pray they will influence the world around them, rather than let it influence them.*

We spent two weeks in Auckland on our way out. Within

two hours of landing in Auckland, Fraser had to sit his driver's licence road test, as this was the only available time before we left the country. But, in an unfamiliar car on unfamiliar roads, he managed to pass.

On the following Saturday, the extended family and friends held a special birthday celebration for Delwyn's mother, who was turning 80. A highlight was reconnecting with Delwyn's two sisters (long since living in Europe—in fact we had not seen either Helen or Ethne for a dozen years, and Ethne's husband, Mark, for even longer). Delwyn had arranged some musical items, which she and her four siblings performed in honour of their mother. It was a special time. As part of the family reunion, we enjoyed day trips to the Auckland SkyTower, the zoo and Waiheke Island before we once again scattered to our various corners of the globe. So ended our last home assignment. Our final field term was about to begin.

## 20

# Through the Waters, Through the Fire

Everyone remembers where they were when they heard the news. September 11, 2001. We were just seven weeks back in the Philippines and still getting back to normal routines. But, like all our in-town colleagues, we rushed over to the office to watch the horrifying images on the news broadcasts. The world had changed.

With the American military response came inevitable threats from terrorist groups and their sympathisers in our part of the world. Our American colleagues based in Indonesia were almost all evacuated, while we in the southern Philippines were in lockdown mode with credible threats from the Abu Sayyaf group. Our crisis management committee looked at possible evacuation scenarios, should that become a necessary situation. We were several days without water as the city made safeguards against an attack on the water supply.

While we were concerned with general safety in these troubled times, we were also much in prayer for Martin and Gracia Burnham, a missionary couple who had been kidnapped along with a number of others by Abu Sayyaf shortly before our return to the Philippines. We never met them but felt an affinity with them as they were about our age, had two boys and a girl, like us, and were celebrating their anniversary at a beach, as we were wont to do, when they were captured. Day after day for many months Delwyn's journal records prayers from the heart for their witness while in captivity and their swift release from it. Many of the other hostages were released after ransoms were paid; a few were beheaded. Martin and Gracia were held for over a year before the final gunfight and release—Gracia to her family, Martin to his Lord in glory.

Between the periods of heightened safety consciousness, there were times when tensions had died down enough for normal life to resume. This included outings for our children and their friends. One of the favourite activities for several of the young people among the expat community was to spend a night or two in the branches of a huge banyan tree on Samal Island. After catching a boat across to the island, the young folk caught motorcycle taxis to a village. A short walk brought them to the tree where they climbed any of its many aerial roots to hang their homemade hammocks between branches. So vast was this tree that 20 people could easily find hanging space without getting in another's way. The arboreal campers generally cooked their meals on a fire at the base of the tree, but I heard that on at least one trip some cooking was even done up in the branches. (I joined them on one of these outings and spent a very comfortable night in my hammock.)

The other hugely popular activity among the teenagers was to go tubing down the Davao River. Conditions could vary hugely. After a dry spell the river flow might only be three kilometres per hour, meaning a long, slow trip with many a bump on rocks; after heavy rains, well…

The overnight rain had been significant after three rather wet days and on January 4th the young people were pumped about how fast the downstream trip would be. Our parental concern was assuaged by the adult leader who assured us that he and the more experienced tubers would make a safety assessment before they committed themselves at the launching point many kilometres upstream. The narrower parts of the river further downstream turned out to be far swifter than their initial calculation, and the flow through these was over 25 kilometres per hour. Eddies and vortexes were wider and deeper than usual, standing waves were up to three metres high and river islands had mostly disappeared—only the tops of trees and bamboo remaining as evidence of their submerged presence, with the main flow now passing dangerously through these groves. Logs and whole clumps of bamboo were also floating downstream, some getting tangled among the submerged trees and thus creating logjams. A constant musical chiming of boulders crashing against one another could be heard as they rolled ever seawards.

Fraser was caught in a wide eddy early on and pulled under by the vortex, before resurfacing and going around and down a second and third time. Eventually he managed to scramble onto the debris piled against an embankment. Knowing the others would be far downstream by now and that it would be foolish to get back into the river alone, he crossed some farmland until he found a road, hitched a lift on a motorcycle to a nearby town and phoned the office to let us know he was alive and ask us to do all we could to get the others out of the river as soon as possible.

For the next couple of hours, the front members of the group were hurtling downstream, with a mix of exhilaration and fear at their speed, unaware of what was happening to those behind them. Isaac was worried all this time, as his last view of his brother was of Fraser being sucked under. Fraser was concerned also for the rest of the party. His last view of his brother was just Isaac's bike helmet behind a wave. Keith, our director at the time, had a motorcycle and took off to see if he could find the group at any one of the riverside villages. By now, those at the front had decided it was too dangerous to continue downstream and managed to scramble ashore with the

*Songs on the Journey*

help of local villagers on the bank. It was exactly at this point that Keith showed up and was able to reassure a very shaken group that Fraser, the only one unaccounted for, was safe.

We later discovered that these were the worst floods for 30 years. The river burst its banks nearer the city. Bridges cracked—one collapsed. Houses were flooded—a pastor we knew lost everything with the water up to the ceiling of his house. The local crocodile farm was swamped and lost many of its residents. Worst of all, several people drowned that day. We are so thankful that none of our young people was among them. We are thankful too that their prayer lives were strengthened through the experience. (By the way, this was not their last tubing trip down the river.)

The translation work continued apace with Uja and Äto' coming for a few months during which we revised II Corinthians, I & II Peter and Jude, and checked Hebrews, I Corinthians and the rest of *Life of Moses* with a consultant.

Later Äto' returned with Iyä, who had been with us in the Philippines four and a half years earlier. It was not until he got off the plane in Davao and was told that he had to get right back on and leave, that he realised there was less than the mandatory six months left on his passport. He had been through quite a deal to arrive, and further delays might have sent him all the way back to the village. He had left his work like a Galilean fisherman when he was called to come (including rice unharvested, a house he had half finished building and his workers who were chain sawing logs for him in the forest that day). After I pleaded with immigration officials and we made a phone call to the Indonesian Consulate in Davao, Iyä was permitted to stay. Next day he had a brand-new passport and the checking he came to assist with could proceed. By the time he left for home we had completed checks of John, Ephesians, Philippians, II Corinthians, I & II Peter and Jude.

Much of Delwyn's time was still spent in teaching music to the elementary school pupils, with all the extra events that entailed. After she led a 23-member community orchestra for a Christmas carol service, we worked together on another musical, this time performed by the middle-schoolers. It was called *Choices* and had a theme of peer pressure.* The open-sided covered basketball court at school was again the venue and again provided its challenges with torrential rain during rehearsals and a failed sound system for the second performance for children of the local community. At least the first performance went off without a hitch.

The focus of the next two months was our trip back to the village area in Indonesia. It was good once there to catch up with so many friends again, but there was a lot of sad news. Two of our close friends told of how they had recently lost children in childbirth, and a third told of how her baby had died at three months after she almost died herself due to a long-delayed delivery of the placenta. Apparently, another lady had died with her child a month earlier in Langsa', and another friend of ours who had delivered twins by herself some years ago had just lost another child. Once again, we longed for medical help to be available in the community.

It was not an easy trip, and we were discouraged at times by the attitude of a couple of people to the translated Word. But there were also some really uplifting times of fellowship and encouragement from folk who were clearly reading regularly and growing through it. Delwyn wrote:

*Thank You, Lord! This family has blessed us again and it has brought tears to my eyes to realise that these are people who value the Word in their language. Then, as I read*

---

\* See song: 'Prayer' (one of the songs from *Choices*)

*the story of Jehoshaphat, I'm reminded again that it is the Lord's work, and He is in control. It takes the pressure off, and we can rejoice in His faithfulness.*

Of all the many visits that trip, the most special for us were those with Indo Bonnäng. She was a poor, elderly lady who was very hard of hearing. She loved to read and devoured the translated portions already produced. And she passed on what she had learned. "Did you know," she asked, "that Jesus can heal people? I read about it. So, when I can't sleep because my leg twitches, I pray, and it settles down so I can sleep." She also asked us if we thought it would be okay if she read the Bible in church during the sermon because she couldn't hear what was being said anyway. We told her we thought it was a great idea.

On the way to the village, we had spent a little time in Tomohon where Delwyn had the opportunity to lead a short seminar on using traditional and locally written music in a worship context. It was attended by some 30 leaders from various churches. She was a little worried about the rustiness of her Indonesian language ability, but she did fine. On the way back to the Philippines we again stopped in at Tomohon and were encouraged by comments sparked by the seminar.

We were about to head to the airport when we heard that not only was the flight cancelled, but the whole service was now suspended and the return tickets we held were now worthless! Our visitor visas were due to expire in a week's time, so we would have to leave the country. And our Philippine visas were almost due for renewal within the Philippines, so if we did not get back there within a week, we would have to start the process anew from outside the country! And who knows how long that might take? There was no other option but to fly to Singapore, then on to Manila, then down to Davao: 5,680 kilometres instead of the usual 640 kilometres and costing an extra US$3,000.

Pin Yoon, a colleague from Singapore, picked us up from the airport, took us out for a meal and put us up for the night in his cousin's apartment during our transit in Singapore. We felt so looked after and blessed by his hospitality. Twelve days after leaving the village we arrived back home in Davao. It was great to be back finally, but the battle with the airline to recoup even a small refund of the return leg of the original ticket left us in knots for two weeks. We calculated that Esther would have to be home-schooled the following year to make up some of the financial shortfall. However, the school principal very generously waived her fees for the following year. He figured that it was worth it to have Delwyn continue in teaching music at the school.

Alongside that, Delwyn spent some time each week cataloguing activities and materials related to local music for each of the 16 language teams working from Davao and encouraging our co-translators and other Indonesian men with indigenous worship. She also worked with an IT specialist to produce a font for printing the musical notation system used throughout Indonesia. This meant we could print written music for any translated hymns or new songs being written. It was later replaced by a more user-friendly system after we left, but for our purposes at the time it functioned well.

I also was temporarily roped into teaching. Due to a teacher shortage, I was asked to take the British Literature classes for our high schoolers. It was only for one semester, and I loved the experience, but, as our director pointed out when he reluctantly asked me to step in, "It is not what you are here for."

Writing musicals was not what we were there for either, but it was a wonderful way of working together on a task we both enjoyed in the evenings. And it provided the school with Christmas and/or May (end of year) productions tailored to the group, rather than buying something pre-packaged. For

Christmas that year we wrote *Papa Martyn's Christmas*, reworked from an earlier version we had written eight years before and based on Tolstoy's story 'Where Love is, There God is Also'.

In the weeks prior to the US-led war in Iraq, we continued to hear of atrocities in parts of Indonesia, including Sulawesi, where Christians were being singled out for execution by radical Islamists. Mostly this was in the Maluku Islands and then in Central Sulawesi near where colleagues' language projects were based, but there were also some disturbances in the part of the island nearer Tabulahan. Meanwhile in the southern Philippines there were further incidents: bombings in Zamboanga and other parts of Mindanao, and then a deadly attack at the Davao airport.

A bomb was left in an outdoor covered area, where hundreds were waiting for passengers to arrive from Manila. It was a place we had often waited to meet guests arriving from overseas, or for our own children coming back from outdoor education or other trips. The blast killed 19 people outright and injured another 140, including a baby from the Southern Baptist mission who was rushed to hospital with shrapnel in his liver. Also, a missionary from the same mission later died from his injuries, adding to the death toll.

A second bomb went off four weeks later at the ferry terminal, killing another 15 people and injuring a further 40. Two days later, I was to head to Indonesia for three weeks for the Bible Society final checks of the Tabulahan New Testament. Less than a week later, Delwyn was to head to Thailand for a consultant training seminar. This did not feel like a good time to be away from each other, let alone from the children. We prayed for them to grow through this time of separation and entrusted them to the Lord.

## 21

# Final Checks

We had now drafted the whole New Testament and portions of the Old, checked every passage for accuracy and, in the village area, for naturalness and for comprehension. Each book had been checked with a consultant and revisions made at each juncture. There remained now the final check with the Indonesian Bible Society who were to be the publishers.

Their offices are located in Bogor, a two-hour bus trip from Indonesia's capital on the island of Java. First, there were three flights to get us there. Thankfully, the Davao-Manado flight service had been reinstated. I met up with Äto' and Uja in Manado and we travelled together the rest of the way. For these two men who were by now used to international travel, this was their first excursion to any of Indonesia's thousands of islands other than their own home of Sulawesi. Äto' was busy nearing the end of his theology degree but was given leave to assist with these checks. Uja was due to begin his theology degree in the near future, so the timing worked out well.

For the next three weeks we re-examined many passages that had been translated. In addition to the two Indonesian Bible Society consultants, an English-speaking international consultant was there at the time, so the questions were directed to us in either Indonesian, which five of us understood, or English, which four of us understood, and our answers were given in both languages. Uja, Äto' and I mostly held discussions in Tabulahan, as this was our normal mode of communication. Consequently, as each day wore on and tiredness took its toll, there were times when I addressed Uja or Äto' in English, the international consultant in Indonesian and the Indonesian consultants in Tabulahan! Everyone was very understanding—at least when the mistake was realised, and the right language employed. It was a full and tiring three weeks, but very necessary. The consultants came up with some helpful suggestions which improved the finished translation.

Meanwhile, Delwyn was in Thailand for consultant training seminars. Members from countries across Asia had been selected for training in their chosen discipline(s). Delwyn took part in the Scripture-in-Use and ethnomusicology sessions. She gained a lot from the sessions and loved meeting up again with her mentors from the Dallas course, Todd and Mary. Also, each afternoon she was glad to be of help to Ajang, an ethnomusicology student from Indonesia, by translating for him during classes so he could actively participate.

Just before Delwyn and I left for Indonesia and Thailand respectively, the high schoolers were excited by a special find. Up to this point the small high school had been held in a rented house. Now there were plans for a new high school building next to the SIL office. As the scrub-covered ground was being cleared, the workmen came across three snakes, the largest of which was a 4.5-metre python (unusually large in urban surroundings and probably responsible for a few missing pets). Though they would not be there once the building was completed, Fraser and Isaac took on the task of preserving the skin for future display at the new school building. However, they were about to head off for 'Outdoor Ed', so left the skin soaking in brine. I'm sure our house helper, Trinnie, who hated snakes, was not impressed for the next week each time she opened the fridge.

*Final Checks*

By the time Delwyn and then I arrived back in Davao, the snakeskin was out of the fridge, tanned and returned to school. It was a wonderful feeling being back together as a family. The children did not seem any the worse for two weeks without Mum and three weeks without Dad. Just as well, because in a month we were to be leaving the two boys behind once more.

We were both sent as delegates to the biennial Indonesia Branch conference—this year to be held in Bali. Delwyn was asked to lead the worship sessions. The theme of the conference was to be 'In His Strength, For His Glory'. Of course, this inspired another song.*

We decided to take Esther along with us rather than leaving her with friends again. The boys were happy to remain in Davao as they were part way through SCUBA courses which they had saved up for by teaching younger children piano (under Mum's supervision). Ever since returning from Thailand Delwyn had been having heart arrhythmia problems. Though medical tests showed there was nothing to worry about, they were quite unsettling, especially for the duration of our time away.

Normally at that time of year, with the children off school for two months, we would return to Tabulahan for village community contact and for checking of translated materials. These days we could only get a one-month visa to be in the country, instead of the previous two-month visitor visa. The conference had severely cut into available village time, so heading there from Bali was not feasible. And after returning to Davao there would be little time for a quick turnaround. Furthermore, the remaining checking still to be done was not village checking, but rather scouring the final draft for inconsistencies. However, there were still a few weeks before school resumed.

* See song: 'In His Strength, For His Glory'

When I asked the children what we should do with the rest of their vacation, Isaac came up with the bright idea that we should build a boat. This seemed like a worthwhile project to me, especially as there were no woodworking classes at either Esther's or the boys' schools. Besides, I possessed both a hammer and a saw—what could be difficult about building a boat? And plans? Who needs plans? So, armed with tape measure and naivety, we set to work.

The initial thought was to build a small Philippine-style *bangka*—a canoe with two outriggers. We decided that marine ply was too expensive. We would make do with ordinary ply and marine paint. Guessing the future beam width based on my hips, we set about making some plywood bulkheads. To these we attached some stringers to make a boat-shaped skeleton. Then, with a mix of trial-and-error-cutting, glue, nails, a lot of brute force followed by a generous application of builders' fill, we skinned it. It looked somewhat boat-shaped and not entirely unlike a steep-sided canoe, or even the main hull of a *bangka*. However, it was now too narrow to accommodate an adult. We had another think and decided to duplicate it and call it a catamaran. A welder at a roadside stall made up a tubular frame to connect the two hulls. The mast and boom were bamboo poles from the market. Delwyn sowed a mainsail and a gib from some nylon material and then a webbing 'trampoline' to span the gap. Esther assisted with painting.

We had a car, but no trailer. In fact, it was rare to ever see one in Davao at that time. Instead, I went back to the welder and commissioned a roof rack. With the car at only four and a half feet wide and the catamaran at seven feet wide, the ungainly load was an unusual sight and turned many heads as we drove through the streets for its maiden voyage. Before we had rigged it on the sand at a local beach, some passers-by, unused to the sight of a catamaran asked, "What is that? Is that an airplane?" No, it would never fly, but it did float and, what is more, sail with some degree of control from the twin rudders. In fact, it was so buoyant that it could hold all five of us, and on subsequent trips, gear and supplies for an overnight on nearby Samal Island.

Besides the sailing, part of the fun was thinking up ways of improving it (and/or repairing it) after each outing. We replaced the initial mast with a longer one, adding an extra panel of sail. Unfortunately, the extra downward pressure caused the welded frame to buckle while out at sea and we limped back to shore, leaving the girls to take a public 'pump boat' back to the mainland. Once refitted with stronger pipework, it sailed well. We sometimes noticed a few little borer holes appearing in the hulls. So *that* was the difference between marine ply and the cheap stuff! Never mind, a bit of filler and a lick of paint kept it seaworthy.

Later, when our time to leave the Philippines approached, we wondered if we would be able to find a buyer for this unusual craft, not that it had cost a lot. There were no takers at our garage sale, but in the end a kind member of the missionary community took it off our hands, saying he would find a use for it somewhere. A year or two later we heard that it was being used to carry Bibles to some of the villages of Samal Island. We could not have wished for better!

When not messing about in boats, and especially after the children were back in school, I continued to pore over the Tabulahan Scriptures, reading and re-reading to check for consistency and accuracy in details like chapter and verse numbers, capitalisation, punctuation, paragraphing, quotation margins, cross-references, parallel passages and key terms. On one of these read-throughs, I discovered an apostrophe (representing a glottal stop consonant) in a place it did not belong. To have left this pre-resurrection verse uncorrected would have rendered "Jesus' corpse" as "Jesus' deputy"! Also, all the field codes for formatting had to be checked before the manuscript could be made 'camera-ready' for the printshop. In the group office Barbara Altork worked tirelessly on getting the manuscript exactly as it needed to be.

Then, finally, on a day in November, it was ready to be sent away to Bogor to be printed. With joy at this news, Delwyn based a song of gratitude on part of the day's Bible reading.

*Not to us, O Lord, not to us but to your name be the glory, because of your love and faithfulness.* (Psalm 115:1)

She later updated a version of this after the Scriptures were published and distributed.*

We both felt so thankful to have reached this point. It had been a tiring and mentally taxing few months. Again, working on writing musicals together in the evenings was a welcome break.

In fact, we worked on two musicals simultaneously. That Christmas the high schoolers put on a musical called *Nick of Time*—a time-travel adventure in which the historical St. Nicholas, bishop of Myra, is brought to the present by some teenagers before they manage to get him home via a detour to Bethlehem in time for the first Christmas.**

A few months later the middle-schoolers performed our final musical: *Father's Heart,* the storyline of which interwove several other parables around the parable of the prodigal son (in our musical's case: the prodigal daughter).*** Once again it was wonderful to see the whole thing coming together so

---

\* See song: 'Not To Us'
\*\* See song: 'In Your Good Time' (one of the songs from *Nick of Time*)
\*\*\* See song: 'Father's Heart' (theme song from *Father's Heart*)

well with the participation of many of our school community. Unfortunately, the first night's performance had to be abandoned mid-way as a lightning storm caused a blackout over the whole city. The second night the weather was perfect, and every member of the cast brought something extra. Though not our prime reason for being there, we wanted to honour the Lord through each of these productions as offerings of worship.

Between those two musicals Delwyn and I were back in Indonesia, leaving the children in the care of Esther's teacher and long-time family friend, Janine Meisner. There were two reasons for this short trip.

First, Delwyn was scheduled to lead a longer song writing seminar in Tomohon. The 30 participants for this came from half a dozen language groups of North Sulawesi. Most were church leaders or elders from their respective churches. Delwyn felt privileged, though a little daunted, to be addressing so august a group. She feared her Indonesian language ability was not up to the task after living principally in the Philippines for ten years. Again, her stress-induced heart arrhythmia played up. But she need not have worried. She communicated well the value of using both the vernacular tongue and the traditional music styles to produce modern songs of worship. The participants composed and enthusiastically performed several songs before the seminar's end.

Second, we wanted to discuss plans for the forthcoming Scripture dedication with the Tabulahan translation committee in the village area. This would be best held in July when the rice harvest was in. There were many questions. How much meat would we need? Who would pay for it? What was the current price for a buffalo, anyway? And when would invitations be sent out? There should be representatives from the Bible Society, the church leadership, SIL Indonesia, WBT NZ, our home church, as well as each Tabulahan-speaking congregation, including those from another denomination. And how and when would we transport the printed Bibles to the area?

We should have known from past experiences that, though we decided all these matters in those few days, it did not mean that any of them would be carried out before we returned in July.

## 22

# New Testament Dedication

In the ensuing three months life continued to be busy, especially for Delwyn, who was also battling a virus for several weeks that caused constant vertigo. Her journal records the busyness and the solution to the stresses of a full schedule:

> *I'm pretty happy with the way [Father's Heart] is coming together, but with the Seko men (translators from another language group) here wanting pointers on song writing, a recording workshop, newsletter to get out and the other ordinary things of life, it has been a little crazy. Last night I realised again as I read Jeremiah 29 that in order to know the future and the hope God promises us we need to seek Him with all our hearts, and that is my longing—to continue to press in close to Jesus in everything, whether I'm busy or not. I am pathetic without Him, insecure and depressed. Even as I turned to Matthew's Gospel today, I felt a relief and a comfort to draw strength again from the Word. Yet, at the same time, the many tasks awaiting me want to drag me away—a reminder of the battle for our souls, whatever guise the distraction may be, even worthy causes. Nothing is worth more than this precious time of coming aside and just being still for a time to draw closer to Jesus.*

## Songs on the Journey

By the time we left for Indonesia in July we had downsized the accumulation of 11 years based in one country. This meant that there would be relatively few things to sort on our return from the Scripture dedication in the village before we said our final goodbyes and attempted to reconnect with our homeland.

We had hoped that Uja would have been able to get the boxes of the translated Word from Ujung Pandang to Tabulahan and had left him funds to do so. However, on arrival two weeks before the dedication we found that the boxes were still sitting there. Hiring a small bus seemed the best option, in that a bus could transport our party as well as the cargo. Janine had come with us from the Philippines, Äto' and his wife Anti' had joined us in Manado, and Uja in Ujung Pandang. The night before we were to meet the bus to begin the journey north, we felt very unsettled and prayed fervently against spiritual oppression. Delwyn hardly slept that night.

Three hours into the journey the next day our bus was flagged down by police. Our immediate concern was that it could be impounded, and an investigation might have led to some awkward questions, like what were a group of foreigners on visitor visas doing carting Bibles around? It turned out to be a minor misunderstanding as to what class of vehicles could use a particular street and they let the driver off with a donation of 'cigarette money'. Our initial concerns about the driver turned out to be misplaced. In fact, even though he had never travelled on the hilly inland road to Lakähäng, he was careful and the best driver we ever engaged.

Just before we went out of range of cell phone coverage to head inland, we received the devastating news that Jon, the eldest son of our dear friends Don and Shari, had passed away in hospital following a terrible boating accident. Jon had been such an encouragement to Fraser over the years as a 'big

## New Testament Dedication

brother' and mentor. We had seen him growing up from a young boy to a gifted and godly young man. His life had been an inspiration to us and no doubt to many others. We were all in shock and Fraser was extremely upset.

We arrived in Lakähäng tired but thankful after 14 hours and unloaded the boxes into the wide front room of Iyä's house. Iyä treated us royally, providing us with mattresses, bedding and mosquito nets, while he slept on a piece of plastic on the concrete, surrounded by cartons of the Word that he had selflessly helped produce.

The following day we hiked upstream to the villages of Tabulahan. While stopping in at the home of our first village host to wait out some light rain, we were treated to a mini concert of songs from a group of Tabulahan children. Some of these songs were ones Delwyn had composed and left on earlier visits. Just before nightfall we reached our adopted household in Salu Leäng, where we were to stay for most of the following two weeks.

Next to nothing had been initiated for the Scripture dedication since the planning session earlier in the year, so it was just as well that we arrived with a week and a half to spare. Although this was our major focus for these days, committee members took on responsibilities for various aspects of the celebrations, leaving us with plenty of time to visit with several of the congregations, with many individuals and to play host to our visitors from overseas when they arrived.

Planning for the various events was proceeding well when, three days before the dedication, we heard the news that two significant people would not be able to be there. Two highly respected teachers: Mama Maya and Mama Tato' had been called to Lakähäng to meet with the district head of education with a view to becoming school principals. This was a very important meeting for their careers and, hence, for their wider families. But, to us at least, their presence at the dedication was highly prized. Mama Maya was one of the translation committee members, and Mama Tato' was the very same Mariones who had been the single most helpful person in getting the project off the ground in the first place. We understood that she could not be in two places at the same time, but we so wanted to honour her at the dedication. It was a hard blow, prompting some lack of sleep and a lot of prayer.

Fraser and Isaac left that same day for Lakähäng to meet guests arriving from New Zealand. David and Karen Baird (our missions pastor), Murray Close and his daughter, Susanna, came from our home church. Ian and Tania Vail came as representatives of WBT NZ, having just transitioned to working again in Indonesia. The following day they all arrived in the main village of Tabulahan, where we joined them to be billeted for the last couple of days. Later that day Joel Garrison (representing our office in Davao) arrived via a little-used jungle route from attending the neighbouring Bambam Scripture dedication three days earlier. Unfortunately, Scott Rempel, who had intended to come with him, was sick in the Bambam area and had to return to Davao.

It was heart-warming to catch up with all these friends with news from afar, especially those we had not seen for several years. But the best news of the day was that the upcoming education meeting in Lakähäng was cancelled and therefore Mama Maya and Mama Tato' would be able to take part in Monday's celebrations. Hallelujah! Thank You, Lord.

On the night before the dedication, the celebrations began with an evening of competitions: first choral group and solo singing, and then Bible reading. The various choral groups had really made an effort in making colourful uniforms as well as in blending voices. Many of the soloists were singing either their own spin on songs Delwyn had written, or new

## New Testament Dedication

creations they themselves had come up with. This so warmed our hearts to see that some of the younger generation were keen to be creative in this way and use their own language to express praise and worship. I was thrilled too to hear how well many of the young people were reading the Word in their own language with thoughtful phrasing. It was quite late that night before everyone retired to bed.

In the morning Mama Indah dressed Delwyn in the traditional women's outfit, while Papa Näi' dressed me in traditional men's garb. Then these respected village elders led us and our guests from Mama Tahe's house to the church. Before we arrived, we were met by two young men who performed a traditional men's dance, before stepping aside to allow us through two lines of female dancers and the throng of people gathered outside the church. The inside of the church was already packed with guests from other villages further afield.

Uja and Äto' did a great job introducing the various speakers, from government representatives to cultural heads, to church leaders, including Karen, our home church missions pastor. I had the honour of interpreting for her before giving my own thoughts.

It was hard to sum up the 15 years of coming and going since that first trip with the family, the valued relationships formed with so many Tabulahan people, the privilege we felt to have been a part of this community and to have been so welcomed by them. I wanted them to know that they were smarter than they often thought themselves. They were our teachers. I wanted to clarify some points on what goes into a meaningful translation. Mostly, I wanted to encourage them to take the Word of the Lord into their hearts, now that they had it in written form.

A visiting pastor gave a good and rousing sermon, mostly in Tabulahan, his wife's language. Following prayers of dedication, the first copies were presented to committee members, our co-translators and other key people in the project. We were so pleased that Mama Tato' (Mariones) was among these.

Following the dedication service, everyone enjoyed a festive meal of buffalo meat and rice. The weather stayed dry throughout the day which was another blessing as the meal preparations were held outdoors, as was the meal itself for many attendees.

The following day, our final day there, we took our overseas guests to visit the hamlets of Salu Leäng and the village of Langsa'. There were so many people we met along the trail, as well as in their homes, who were probably just so many faces to our visitors, but of whom we could tell stories of past interactions, of laughs and tears and sharing. Again, we were struck with the privilege we had had to be a part of these peoples' lives. In Kombeng we met Papa Näi' who expressed that God's Word is like gold, but not gold that can be stolen; when it is in your heart it can't be taken away. We pray that more and more of his fellow villagers will take the Word to heart and find life through it.

It poured with rain that night, so the trail out the following day was somewhat muddy, prompting more than a few slips. In Lakähäng Iyä had a meal ready and two vans lined up to take us and our guests to Mamuju. We were late arriving there, but in time to book seats on the night bus. We hoped the bookings would not have filled before then. In fact, there were exactly the right number of empty seats for our party. Faithful Lord, thank You once again!

We had received sad news at this point on our way in. Now again we received sad news on our way out. Äto' had to break the news he had just heard to his wife, Anti', that her mother had passed away. We were shocked. We had met her in Manado two weeks earlier and she seemed in good health, the same age as Delwyn. Anti' confirmed it via phone call and was distraught. Delwyn sat and comforted her as we waited the two hours for the bus. Äto' and Anti' would now have the care of her five siblings, the youngest being just two years old. A few days later in Manado we visited the grave and heard that Anti's mother had died as a result of a fall after fainting in the bathroom, as so nearly happened to Delwyn six years before.

We had the best part of a day in Ujung Pandang with our overseas guests before we took our various flights. The highlight of this was meeting up again with Neri, the first believer we were aware of from the Aralle dialect of the language, whom we had met at the home of friends back in February. Karen was keen to meet her and asked about her testimony. John 14:6 figured strongly in this. ("*I am the way, the truth and the life. No one comes to the Father except through me.*") We gave her two copies of the Tabulahan Scriptures. Neri expressed how hard it had been talking with relatives about the gospel using terms from the Indonesian Bible. Now she would be able to read directly to them from the Tabulahan and they could understand. Isaac mentioned that Acts 4:12 is a bit like John 14:6. She turned to it and began to read Paul's words in her language. *"Salvation is found in no one else, for there is no other name under heaven given to men by which we must be saved."*

"This is so clear!" she said. "I will be able to use this to explain things to my family." It was truly the best moment of the year for me.

And so, our time in Indonesia came to an end. What a privilege it had been to live among these folk for a season, to learn something of their ways and language. They had welcomed us into their homes and lives. And we were blessed too when hosting the six young men who lived with us in Davao. They became uncles to our children, and younger brothers to Delwyn and me.

Looking back, those 17 years overseas seem but a blink. They were frequently the most difficult days of our lives, but also the most fulfilling. There were many hurdles, but the Lord helped us over each one of them. There were many lessons learned, with many more still to learn. There were people who rubbed us up the wrong way, as we no doubt were insensitive enough to rub others up the wrong way. But there were many, many more good relationships forged, borne of tears and laughs and working together.

We could not say that many had come to know the Lord in a deeper way through our time among them, but we left the community the best gift we could leave any community: the Word of the Lord in a language they understand. It is the Good Seed. And we trust Him for the increase. As a 'member care' pastor once said to us at a time we were feeling particularly discouraged: "It is God's Word, it *will* impact them." We long to see that happen among the people of Aralle-Tabulahan and beyond. It needs to happen too in each of our lives. May we all be diligent in reading and meditating on the life-giving Word.*

---

* See song: 'Treasure of Ages'

# Epilogue

How quickly the years fly by! It was more than a decade before we returned to Tabulahan.

Fraser had already been back twice in the intervening time. He had been a groomsman for a friend from Malaysia and added an Indonesian leg to the journey to link up with Äto' in Manado and travel with him to Tabulahan. He came back full of stories of those we knew, of village changes, of ideas for helping further. There was now a motorcycle road all the way to the village area and some small-scale hydro-electric generation. Äto' and Anti' had made a video of Tabulahan songs, which Äto' distributed to any household with a television and video player.

It happened that the timing of Fraser's first trip coincided with the audio recording of the Tabulahan New Testament. Two Christian converts from Java, radio technicians with Faith Comes By Hearing, were working at the house of Sone', who had the most reliable electricity set up. They were thrilled to meet Fraser as someone whose family had been so involved with the translation, and Fraser was impressed with how thorough they were at selecting good readers and making sure there was no divergence from the written text. Sone' spent his time shooing away dogs, chickens, motorbikes and other noisy pests during recording. Eventually the audio version of the Tabulahan New Testament was made available through the 'Bible.is' app.

*Songs on the Journey*

On both of Fraser's trips he also spent time in Aralle and found other believers among Neri's extended family, including a couple with a heart for outreach. In Tabulahan he observed that many young people now owned cell phones, not that there was cell phone or internet reception, but it was a simple way to own a camera! This gave him an idea.

When Isaac suggested we all make a trip to Tabulahan because it was high time we did (and so that his wife, Chuana, could fill in that part of his past), we agreed that we should. Fraser then ordered a hundred micro-SD cards and copied the audio New Testament, as well as some of Delwyn's more recent Tabulahan songs, onto them. Once we reached the village area, he found those with cell phones and offered to insert the SD cards so that they could also listen to the Word, and not just use their phones for taking photos.

On the way into the village area, we stayed with Daud and his family, who are now part of a charismatic fellowship in Mamuju. We stayed with Iyä and family on the way through Lakähäng. Iyä had been doing some impressive carpentry and joinery on the church building across from his house, as well as serving as an elder in that congregation. We caught up with Mama Tato' (Mariones), now a grandmother, retired and living in Lakähäng. In Tabulahan we stayed a night or two with Mama Tahe', but mostly with Sone' and family where there was more space. Sone' has some great innovative and entrepreneurial skills which are a model that could benefit the community. He had recently stepped down from church eldership. The house in Salu Leäng where we used to stay is no longer standing. But again, we stayed with Mama Ondong who had moved to Langsa'. While we were there, newly married Uja arrived and brought his wife to be welcomed into the community, a lovely Christian woman from another language group. We also caught up with Ando', now one of the pillars of the community. It was encouraging to see each of these young men who had worked with us in the Philippines being so respected in their roles.

There were those we were sad to miss. Papa Semeng and Mama Ri'na, for example, had passed on. And there were those who were not as strong as we remembered. Mama Semeng was still her wonderful smiley self, though unable to speak due to a stroke. We enjoyed some fellowship with her and her son's family. We also enjoyed spending time with the parents of Ando' in Salu Batu. Sadly, his mother, Mama Emang, was also immobile following a stroke.

But it was wonderful to see the next generation rising up to take their place. Esther's best village friend, Da'ling, was now a midwife and ran a health clinic in the village of Lisu. All the boys' friends were now heads of their own households and taking on social responsibilities. And there was evidence of growing faith among some of these young people. At a young people's meeting we attended one evening I was impressed by the participation of the young folk and in particular a grandson of Papa Näi'. He prayed so fervently, not using Indonesian, as many of the educated do, but with great passion in the Tabulahan language.

May this be the start of a move of the Spirit of the Lord leading these dear ones deeper into all He has for them.

# Appendix 1: Maps

*Appendix 1: Maps*

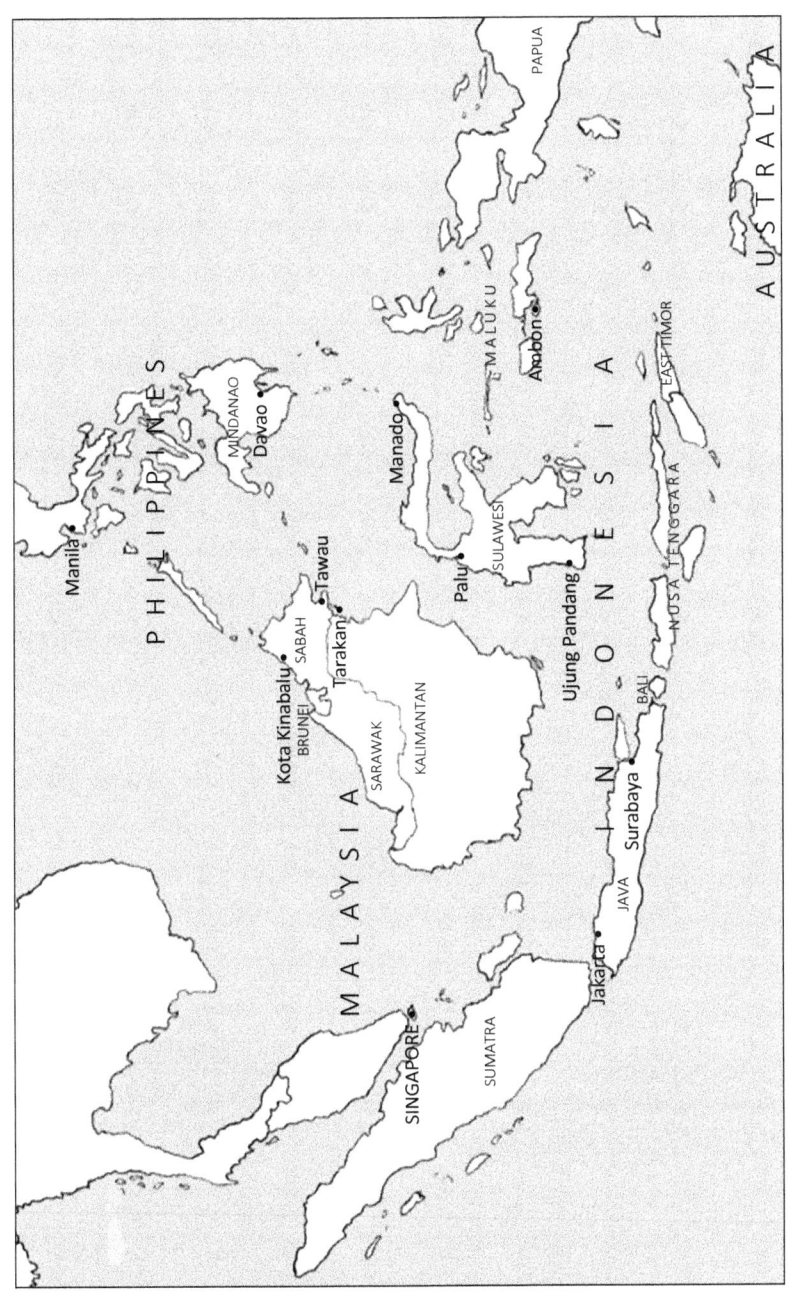

*Map 1: Insular southeast Asia.*

Songs on the Journey

Map 2: Sulawesi, showing towns and roads referred to and current provincial boundaries. (Note: West Sulawesi was part of South Sulawesi during the time of this account.)

*Appendix 1: Maps*

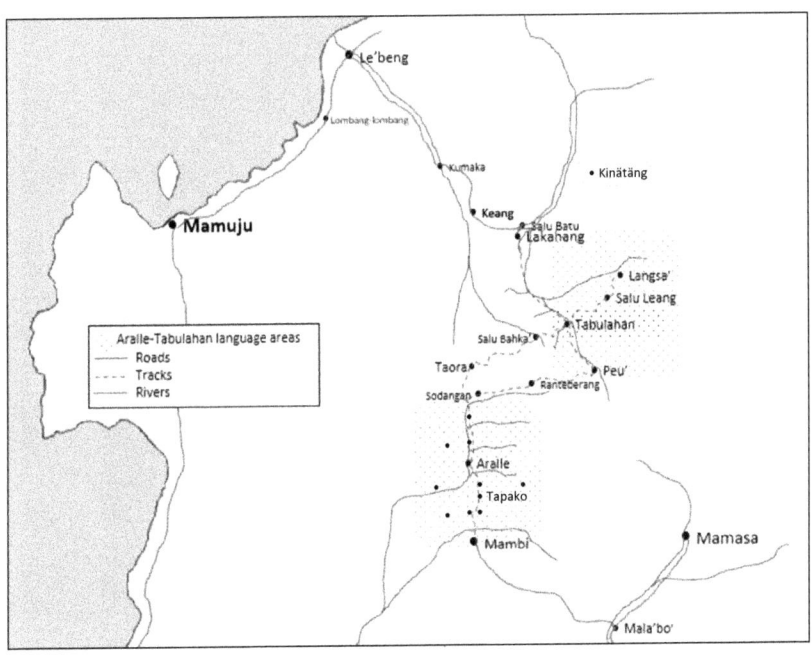

*Map 3: The villages of Aralle-Tabulahan and surrounding area.*

# Appendix 2: Songs

Scan this QR code
with your cellphone or visit
www.wycliffenz.org/songsonthejourney
to hear audio versions
of these songs.

*Appendix 2: Songs*

# Although I Don't Know Why

Copyright © Delwyn McKenzie 1989, 2023

*Songs on the Journey*

# Come Upon These People

Copyright © Delwyn McKenzie 1990, 2023

*Appendix 2: Songs*

*Songs on the Journey*

# Bless the Lord My Soul

Copyright © Delwyn McKenzie 1990, 2023

*Appendix 2: Songs*

# So Much To Be Thankful For

Copyright © Delwyn & Robin McKenzie 2000, 2023

*Songs on the Journey*

## Many Are The Wonders

Lyrics Psalm 40:5  Music: Copyright © Delwyn McKenzie 1991, 2023

*Appendix 2: Songs*

*Appendix 2: Songs*

Songs on the Journey

# Come With Us

Copyright © Delwyn McKenzie 1996, 2023

*Appendix 2: Songs*

*Songs on the Journey*

# When You Pray

Some-where in your day you find a mo-ment.

A thought comes your heart goes out__ and you re-mem-ber me__ in

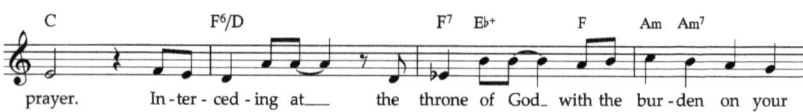
prayer. In-ter-ced-ing at__ the throne of God_ with the bur-den on your

heart, al-though you can - not see it the powers of dark-ness fall a -

part__ for when you pray on the o-ther-side of the world I know God's

pre - sence.__ When you pray__ on the o-ther-side of the world I know God's

Copyright © Delwyn McKenzie 1997, 2023

*Appendix 2: Songs*

*Songs on the Journey*

# Wounds of Love
From the Musical "The Selfish Giant"

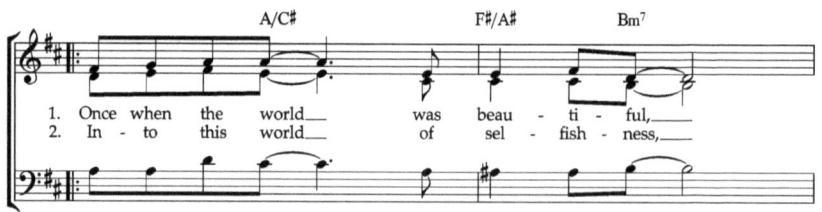
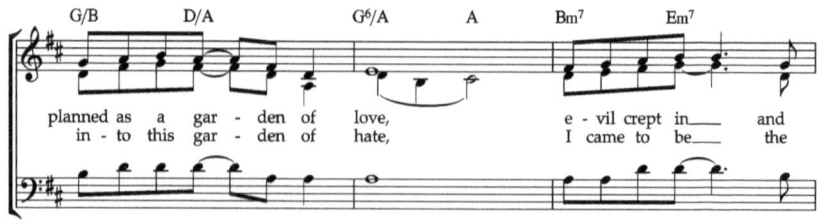

1. Once when the world was beautiful, planned as a garden of love, evil crept in and
2. Into this world of selfishness, into this garden of hate, I came to be the

Copyright © Robin & Delwyn McKenzie from the musical "The Selfish Giant" 1998, 2023

*Appendix 2: Songs*

*Songs on the Journey*

## 142. Kalaena Dehatantaa'

*(2 Tes 3:16)*

do = d   palu 4   MM ± 80

Musik: D McKenzie

*Appendix 2: Songs*

Songs on the Journey

# Dying to Save
From the Musical "Hey Joe!"

Copyright © Robin & Delwyn McKenzie from the musical "Hey Joe!" 2000, 2023

*Appendix 2: Songs*

*Songs on the Journey*

## In His Strength, For His Glory

Copyright © Robin & Delwyn McKenzie 2003, 2023

*Appendix 2: Songs*

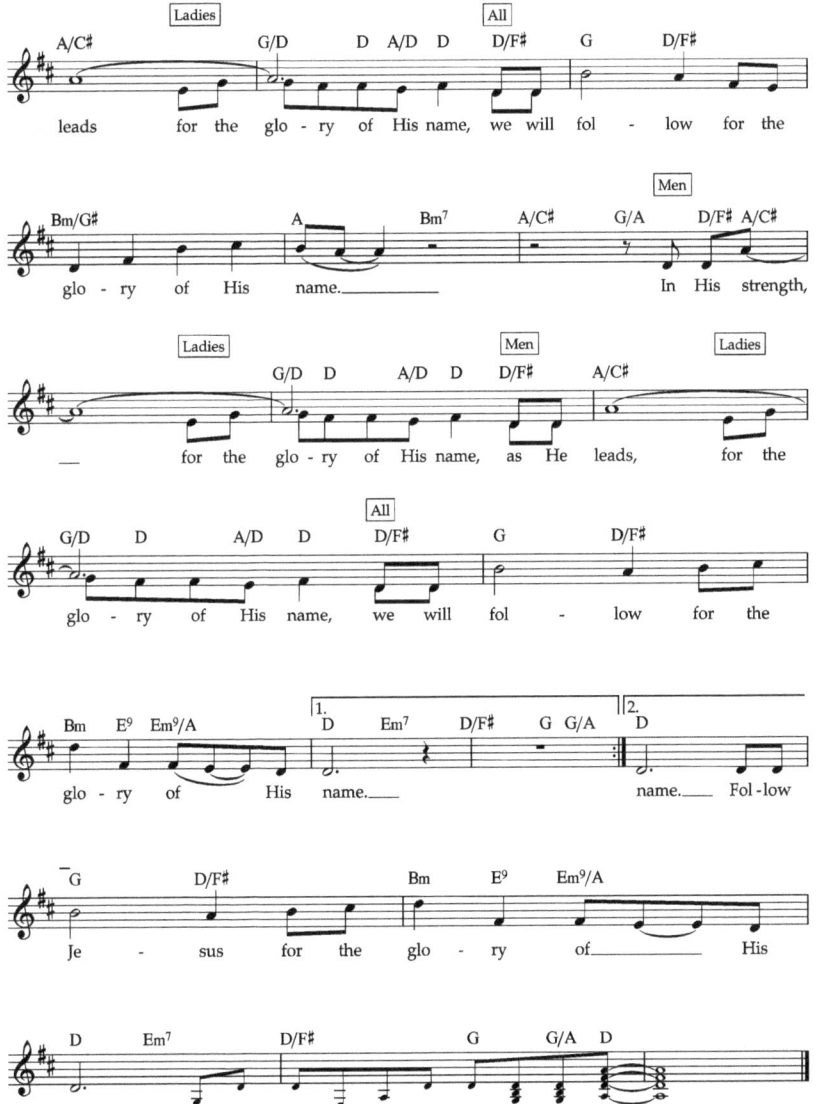

*Songs on the Journey*

# Not to us
### Based on Psalm 115:1

Copyright © Delwyn McKenzie 2004, 2023. Written after the dedication of the New Testament for the Tabulahan people

*Appendix 2: Songs*

*Appendix 2: Songs*

## Treasure of Ages

Copyright © Robin & Delwyn McKenzie 2003, 2023

*Appendix 2: Songs*

www.ingramcontent.com/pod-product-compliance
Lightning Source LLC
Chambersburg PA
CBHW062045290426
44109CB00027B/2739